READING CATULLUS

Of all the Roman poets Catullus is the most accessible to the modern reader. His poems range from the sublimely beautiful to the scatologically disgusting, and from the world of heroic epic poetry to the dirt of the Roman streets.

This introductory book, which assumes no prior knowledge of Roman poetry, explores Catullus in all his many guises. In six concise chapters John Godwin deals with the cultural background to Catullus' poetic production, its literary context, the role of love, Alexandrian learning and the ancient tradition of obscenity and, in the final chapter, he considers the coherence and rationale of the collection as a whole.

The book includes a useful timeline and a guide to further reading. Each chapter is illustrated by readings from the poems chosen to give a representative overview of Catullus' poetry. All Latin is translated.

John Godwin is the Head of Classics at Shrewsbury School. He has edited and translated the complete works of Catullus and is also the author of seven books on Roman poetry.

GREECE AND ROME LIVE

Also available in this series:
Ancient Greece in Film and Popular Culture, Gideon Nisbet (2006;
    second edition 2008)
Augustine: The Confessions, Gillian Clark (2005)
Gruesome Deaths and Celibate Lives: Christian Martyrs and Ascetics,
    Aideen M. Hartney (2005)
Hadrian's Wall and its People, Geraint Osborn (2006)
Hannibal: Rome's Greatest Enemy, Dexter Hoyos (2008)
Julius Caesar, Robert Garland (2004)
The Politics of Greek Tragedy, David M. Carter (2007)
The Tragedies of Sophocles, James Morwood (2008)

Forthcoming titles:
After Virgil: The Poetry, Politics and Perversion of Roman Epic,
    Robert Cowan
Ancient Rome at the Cinema: Story and Spectacle in Hollywood and Rome,
    Elena Theodorakopoulos
Augustus: Caesar's Web: Power and Propaganda in Augustan Rome,
    Matthew D.H. Clark
The Classical Greek House, Janett Morgan
Greek Tyranny, Sian Lewis
The Law in Ancient Greece, Christopher Carey
Pausanias: An Ancient Guide to Greece, John Taylor
The Trojan War, Emma Stafford

READING CATULLUS

John Godwin

BRISTOL
PHOENIX
PRESS

Cover illustration: *Favourite Poet* by Lawrence Alma Tadema, © National Museums Liverpool (Lady Lever Gallery)

First published in 2008 by
Bristol Phoenix Press
an imprint of The Exeter Press
Reed Hall, Streatham Drive
Exeter, Devon EX4 4QR
UK
www.exeterpress.co.uk

Every effort has been made to contact copyright holders in order to obtain permission for use of the illustrations. We would like to take this opportunity to acknowledge any copyright holder that we may have failed to contact.

British Library Cataloguing in Publication Data
A catalogue record for this book is available from the British Library

Paperback ISBN 13: 978 1 904675 64 8
Hardback ISBN 13: 978 1 904675 63 1

Typeset by Carnegie Book Production, Lancaster in Chaparral Pro 11pt on 15pt
Printed in Great Britain by CPI Antony Rowe, Chippenham

To Heather
lux mea, qua viva vivere dulce mihi est

Contents

PREFACE

M ost people who are learning Latin breathe a sigh of relief when they start to read Catullus. Here, after endless accounts of long battles and silly stories about gods, is something and somebody we can actually believe in and relate to. Here is a poet who lived and breathed and was just like us. He appeals to young readers especially because of the dangerous quality of a lot of his verse – Catullus was said to have died young and many of his poems strike a rebellious and provocative note against the old guard running Roman society and writing Roman literature, while also sighing with passion and unrequited love. He boasted that the poetry of his friends would live and travel as far as Cyprus while that of his derivative rivals will end up wrapping fish. He proclaimed his love for a married woman and dared to insult Julius Caesar and Cicero. He suffered the death of his brother and the heartache of being betrayed by his girlfriend, but he also enjoyed parties, uncomplicated sex and lots of laughter. The poems of Catullus are a reminder, if we need one, that Romans in the first century BCE were not a totally different species from the rest of us, and they come over to us even at this distance of time and space as Wordsworth's 'man talking to men'.

Catullus also enjoys notoriety for the exuberant obscenity of some of his verses, and this is an aspect of his work which has only recently been examined in detail. This poet thought nothing odd about writing a plangent 'serious' poem and setting it next to the sort of language we only find as graffiti in Pompeii. He scales the heights and he plumbs the depths like no other ancient writer – and all this in a sequence of poems which only occupy about 80 pages in a modern printed text.

This book is intended for the student or the reader who has not read Catullus before and who would like a general introduction to the poet and his work. It contains quotations from the Latin and (my own) translations of it but it is not intended to be a substitute for the text itself and should be read as an attempt to help others to find the sort of inspiration and pleasure in reading Catullus which I have always found ever since I first laid hands on his poetry at the age of 13.

My debts are many. First of all, to Martin Thorpe who read the book in typescript and who gave generously of his time and scholarship in pointing out the many flaws and errors it contained. He is not responsible for any of the mistakes which remain. My students at Shrewsbury School over the years have allowed me to use them as guinea pigs for some of the ideas in this book and always came up with intelligent reasons why my ideas were probably in need of further development. I also owe a debt of great respect and gratitude to John Betts who commissioned the book in the first place. The academic referee of the University of Exeter Press made a number of acute and helpful suggestions which made the final book a great deal more readable than it would otherwise have been. My greatest debt is to my wife Heather who has put up with me talking about Catullus for far too long and for whom this slender book is but scant recompense for her unstinting love and support. To her the book is dedicated.

John Godwin
Shrewsbury 2008

TIMELINE OF EVENTS AND AUTHORS MENTIONED

---

c. 750–700 BCE	Homer's *Iliad* and *Odyssey*
c. 700 BCE	Hesiod flourishes
c. 650–600 BCE	Sappho born
c. 525 BCE	Aeschylus (tragic poet) born
c. 518 BCE	Pindar born
c. 496 BCE	Sophocles (tragic poet) born
458 BCE	Aeschylus' *Oresteia* produced in Athens
c. 450 BCE	Aristophanes born
431 BCE	Peloponnesian War begins between Athens and Sparta
c. 428 BCE	birth of Plato
404 BCE	Athens defeated in Peloponnesian War
399 BCE	execution of Socrates in Athens
c. 320–305	birth of Callimachus
205–184 BCE	Comedies of Plautus
160s BCE	Comedies of Terence
106 BCE	birth of Cicero
100 BCE	birth of Julius Caesar
90s BCE	birth of Lucretius
c. 84 BCE	birth of Catullus in Verona

70 BCE	birth of Virgil
65 BCE	birth of Horace
59 BCE	birth of Livy
50s BCE	(probably) deaths of Lucretius and Catullus
44 BCE	assassination of Julius Caesar
43 BCE	murder of Cicero
	birth of Ovid
31 BCE	battle of Actium sees Octavian defeat Antony and Cleopatra
30s BCE	Horace, *Epodes*
23 BCE	Horace, *Odes* books 1–3
19 BCE	death of Virgil
8 BCE	deaths of Horace and Maecenas
14 CE	death of Augustus
14–37 CE	principate of Tiberius
c. 38–41 CE	birth of Martial
66 CE	death of Petronius
c. 70 CE	birth of Suetonius
c. 115–30	Juvenal writing *Satires*

CHAPTER 1

A WRITER'S WORLD

The life of Gaius Valerius Catullus is something of a mystery. St Jerome tells us that the poet was born in Verona in 87 BCE and that he died thirty years later. Catullus in his poems refers to known individuals from the period (such as Caesar (poem 93) and Cicero (poem 49)) and speaks (poem 10) of his foreign travel on the staff of the Roman governor Memmius. It seems therefore that he was at least on the lower rungs of the political ladder in his youth and it is quite possible that he was destined for an eminent political career, a career which Ovid suggests (*Amores* 3.9.61) was cut short by an untimely death. He also shows knowledge of Greek and Roman literature in his poetry – he produces some marvellous translations of Greek poetry into Latin verse, such as poems 66 and 51 – and one must therefore assume that he had a privileged education, as only the rich could afford anything more than the most basic of education in the Roman world.

The details of his life will always remains something of a mystery – but it is worth stressing that one should not confuse the historical search for a biography of a writer with anything like a literary assessment of his work. Nor is it any longer normal practice for scholars to use poetry as adequate evidence for the attitudes of 'the Romans' to such things as homosexuality or religion. The difficulties with either the biographical or the documentary approach are obvious. The girl whom the poet addresses as 'Lesbia' has excited the curiosity of every reader of the poems, and yet, for all the time and effort that has been spent on the question, the girl's identity still remains uncertain. The poetry, which uses her name, is written to be part of an artistic collection and not a time capsule to show us a bygone era. This book will focus largely on the literary qualities and merits of the poetry itself.

This is, however, not to say that it is not important to put the text in a historical context of the wider society in which Catullus was living and working, and in particular the audiences about whom and for whom he was writing. In this first chapter I will try to give an outline of some of the salient features of the political and social world of the poet and the way in which his own education and background may have influenced his choice and use of poetic imagery.

So what sort of a society did Catullus live in? One run by and for men, and one run for and by soldiers. A society of celebrities – when the poet sneers at Caesar in poem 93 ('I don't care what sort of man you are') this is provocative only because every citizen in Rome did care what sort of a man Caesar was. A society in which it was accepted to write love poetry to both women and boys but also one in which sexual insecurity was rife. A society in which the writing of poetry was a source of fun as well as an expression of deeper feelings. A world in which there was enough freedom of speech to allow the poet to make scandalously rude allegations about his fellow citizens – something which Juvenal 150 years later sorely misses.

The form of government which Rome had was a republic – ever since the expulsion of the infamous Tarquin the Proud in 510 BCE – which meant that they had no royal family. Power tended to be held by noblemen who had the money and the expertise to canvass and secure election to the magistracies of state each year. It was perfectly possible for new blood to enter the system – Cicero, for instance, whom Catullus addresses in poem 49 as 'most eloquent of

the descendants of Romulus', was the first man in his family ever
to become consul in 63 BCE – but it was far from easy. The top job
in Rome was the consulship; two of them were elected every year,
thus providing both a back-up in case one of them died in office
and also a check by each on the power of his colleague. Below the
consulship were a range of lesser officials all wielding power and
to a greater or lesser extent running Rome and its empire. It was
normal practice to climb the *cursus honorum* ('ladder of offices') and
there were age restrictions which ensured that (for instance) a man
had to sit in the senate for 12 years before being eligible to stand
for the consulship. All well and good – Rome's senior politicians all
had long years of experience of public life and the ways of the world.
The system would be turned upside-down a generation later when
Augustus became the first Roman emperor – but the period when
Catullus was writing his poetry was one in which the old machinery
of checks and balances which had kept the Roman empire growing
for 200 years was still working. There were, however, signs of the
systemic flaws which would ultimately destroy it. The life of Catullus
overlaps with the beginning of the career of Pompey the Great, one
of those army commanders whose control of the legions would lead
them to fight for control of the state. Elections in this period were
increasingly dominated by violence and the old certainties whereby
the landed elite governed the Roman state were suspended. In
Cicero's famous quip, *inter arma silent leges* ('where weapons are out
the laws keep silent').

One aspect of the background to Catullus which is directly
relevant to this book is the mechanics of book production in the
ancient Roman world and the reception of the ancient text by
its contemporary audience. Ancient culture was predominantly an
oral culture. Homer was (probably) an oral performer whose epics
were only written down much later, dramas – tragedy and comedy
– were written to be performed on the stage, oratory (both political,

forensic and also epideictic) was composed for delivery in public. This habit of hearing ancient literature rather than silent reading went beyond these obviously public genres. The historians gave recitations of their work (Livy only attracted small audiences, we are told: Tacitus tells us that audiences wanted to go home with memorable phrases in their minds). So did the poets: Virgil was a formidable performer of his own poetry, reading out the whole of his *Georgics* to the young Octavian over several days in 29 BC, and Juvenal complains that one cannot escape the endless recitations given by poets at parties and in the baths. Audience response, said Aristotle, was the key element in determining the speech's purpose (*Rhetoric* 1358b2–4) and ancient education (at least Higher Education) was, as we shall see, in the main rhetorical education to produce confident and competent public speakers.

Clearly this highly public manner of reception differs vastly from the predominant method employed in modern literary society, where the text is usually taken home and read silently by an individual in private. Reading today is a private matter to stay in for: in the ancient world literature was more often a reason to go out. As Kenney[1] puts it: 'a book of poetry or artistic prose was not simply a text in the modern sense but something like a score for public or private performance', although we do also see evidence of people 'reading' texts to themselves (e.g. Aristophanes, *Frogs* 52–3, and Caecilius' unnamed girlfriend in poem 35). What is notable is that even private reading was not usually silent: when Caesar was found to be reading silently it was commented on as something extraordinary.

Roman poets like Catullus, unlike dramatists or orators, did not have a natural opportunity to display their works in public and so had to arrange readings if they were to have a 'public' at all. They could hire a hall and perform to anybody who cared to come: they could recite their works at dinner parties (as Trimalchio recites verse at his dinner in Petronius' *Satyricon* 55): or they could have their works recited in the baths or even on the street. Reciting poems to a small group of friends and inviting their critical comments was a well-established custom (cf. Cicero, *ad Quintum Fratrem* 3.5; Horace (*Ars Poetica* 386–90) recommends nine years of such informal 'advice' before letting the work loose on a wider public, a recommendation apparently adopted by Catullus' friend Cinna (poem 95)). Publishing in the modern sense of producing multiple copies of a text was of course also done – but the exercise was costly in terms of both money and of needing educated slave copyists. Cicero's friend Atticus was perhaps the first Roman to go into publishing as a business venture, and there were large libraries both private (e.g. that of Piso or Lucullus) and public (the first one being the Pollio library founded in 39 BCE). Poetry could be bought and sold – Horace claims that no bookseller will let *his* poems be mauled by sweaty hands (*Satires* 1.4.71–2) – and might even (horror of horrors) end up as a school textbook (Horace, *Epistles* 1.20.17–18); Propertius (2.34.65–6), for example, speaks of Virgil's *Aeneid* becoming a classic text before Virgil was dead. Catullus (14.17) talks of buying up the works of bad poets from the bookstalls. The advantage of being published in book form is that the writer reaches a much wider audience than recitation could find – libraries were later placed all over the Roman world and carried Roman literature as far as St Albans in 'Furthest Britain' and so Catullus' confidence that Cinna's *Zmyrna* will travel far (poem 95) may not be misplaced or hyperbolic – but had the disadvantage that the author lost control of the reception of his text which might be 'mauled' in performance just as Horace fears the book will be mauled at the bookshop. Horace (as often) puts the matter neatly: *nescit uox missa reverti* – 'once sent out, the voice cannot come back' (*Ars Poetica* 390: cf. *Epistles* 1.20.6, Martial 1.3). Once the text was in the public domain, it became the property of the public and

left authorial control for ever so that anyone who wanted to do so
could get a text copied for himself: plagiarism was an ever-present
danger in a society with no such thing as copyright law, although
(paradoxically) publication did at least assert the authorship of the
text and might actually protect against plagiarism; and the only way
in which corrections could be made to a text once published was to
issue a new text going back on and replacing the earlier one.

Writers throughout the ages have complained of being poorly
paid, and one sometimes wonders why they bothered to have their
work published at all as the financial rewards in the Roman world
were so derisory. Horace (*Ars Poetica* 345) and Martial (10.74.7)
lament the fact that the publisher makes money from their text but
they see precious little of it, and there were really only the following
options for the Roman writer: either enjoy patronage and be paid for
producing work which the patron wanted (or writing poems which
decline to do so (*recusationes*)), such as seems to have happened in
the case of Augustus' friend Maecenas with his generous support
of the poets Horace, Virgil, Propertius and others; alternatively one
could have private income and not need the money; or else suffer
poverty and live off the dole like any other *cliens* (Juvenal 1.134).
Most scholars assume that Catullus fell into the second category:
his educational background and lifestyle seems to have been well-to-
do – although he pleads poverty (13.8) this may simply mean that
he spent beyond his lavish means – and he found himself moving
in the circles of political figures such as Memmius and Caesar. His
dedicatee is Cornelius Nepos but it is generally believed that Nepos
was a literary supporter rather than a financial backer. Wiseman[2]
goes so far as to say: 'Catullus was a man of substance, far from the
necessity of earning patronage by his pen; he wrote for a cultured
élite, and despised the popular taste (95.10).' Catullus was, however,
a provincial from Verona rather than a native Roman, and even if he
had good connections in Verona he would have needed some help

in getting his works known in Rome (as he obviously did from the number of Roman poets who echo him).

Catullus, to be sure, does not refer in his poems to recitation as the mode of reception, but then neither does Virgil. Catullus does refer to his poems being written down as notes on wax tablets (e.g. poems 42, 50) but the tone of these poems makes it clear that the notes are sketches rather than the finished item which was produced as a proper book 'polished with pumice stone' (1.2). The whole point of poem 42 is that the poet is angry that his first draft jottings have left his safe keeping and may be being mocked or copied elsewhere, the additional irony being that this poem is itself a finished product even though it treats of first jottings. We are surely justified in assuming then that the text we have is the finished product and that these poems were to be received by a listener rather than a silent reader of the book.

At the other end of the spectrum from personal poems were works which were specifically composed for the theatre – tragedies, comedies, mimes – and the rhetoric which was written for a specific purpose in the lawcourts or the senate. We all know a bit about tragedy and comedy from modern plays, and we have quite a few comedies from the early republic – the works of Plautus and Terence have survived in quantity and were once far more widely read than they are today. Of Roman tragedy we have very little, which is a huge loss to our appreciation of such poets as Ovid, whose play *Medea* was said to be outstandingly good. We do possess some of the plays of Seneca – but the jury is still out on the question of whether they were composed for the stage or the salon, for dramatic performance with costumes and action or solely for recitation to the imperial court.

Mime was something else entirely. Mime for the Romans was outrageous. The texts that survive are fragmentary and don't sound too exciting – old-hat stories about adulterous wives and wicked servants. What was different about the Mime was that they did not wear masks and so it was much more lifelike, and that they allowed women to play parts on stage. The Romans were far too crafty to miss a trick here, and so Mime was the place where one could see sex on stage, naked actresses and scandalous goings-on. These actresses were not citizen women, of course – no Roman would allow his wife or his daughter to cavort on stage in anything, let alone a sex show. But they were popular for obvious reasons and drew huge crowds to the festivals – notably the Flower Festival (*Floralia*) in the summer. Catullus may have written mimes himself – certainly his poems sit side by side with the outrageous world of the mime on the one hand and the deep drama of tragedy on the other. The ancient book was, then, very much a script rather than a text in itself. Literature was performed rather than imbibed privately. We catch glimpses of poetry being recited at dinners, in the baths, even on street corners, and most publicly of all in the theatre; we see very little of poetry being bought and sold by private individuals for private reading but we hear Juvenal complaining of all the tired derivative epic poetry being poured out into his defenceless ears. We have very few fragments of serious drama from Catullus' day but we know from the letters of Cicero and elsewhere how important the theatre was as a forum for discussion of ideas and expression of feelings.

The survival of the text of Catullus seems something of a miracle – in a world where books are not stored routinely how did we come to have this body of work composed by a man of no political importance? One can imagine how the correspondents of Cicero might have wanted to publish his letters, and how hearers of the *Aeneid* would wish to have a permanent copy of the text – but we know very little of how the 'Book of Catullus' came to be published and in what form. At some point somebody – possibly the poet himself – must have gathered his poems together and put the dedicatory poem 1 at the front to produce what he calls a *libellus* or 'little book'.

In fact the survival of the text is a major fluke. One manuscript of his poems turned up in Verona in the fourteenth century and was copied; all our texts of the poet since then rely on the authority of this one manuscript, which is called V by scholars. Had it not been for V, we would only have poem 62 and a few fragments. Yet Catullus clearly made an impression on those around and after him. A generation later the poet Ovid composes a parody of one of Catullus' most famous poems – Catullus' elegy (poem 3) on the death of his girlfriend's sparrow is turned into Ovid's lament for a dead parrot (*Amores* 2.6) – and parody always presupposes familiarity or the joke falls flat. Virgil even takes a line out of a poem by Catullus in one of the most moving moments of his epic poem *The Aeneid:* the grieving Aeneas pleads that he left queen Dido against his will, saying (6.460) 'unwilling, o queen, did I leave your shore'. Catullus' poem 66 tells the bizarre tale of a lock of hair from queen Berenice of Egypt which flies to the skies and becomes the constellation 'Coma Berenices', leaving the queen with the words (line 39) 'unwilling O queen did I leave your head' (though it is possible that both Catullus and Virgil were here copying a common source). There clearly was an edition of Catullus in circulation not long after the poet's death and his influence on later Latin literature – especially love elegy – was immense.

Finally let us look at the sort of education, which the young Catullus must have had in his home city of Verona, as this in turn gives us some clue as to the academic and rhetorical values of his age.

Roman education was rhetorical. The primary means of all forms of communication was oral and not written and so anyone who aspired to a place of power and influence in the world had to be able to speak effectively in public. Boys practised the art of speech-making by composing speeches on historical themes – an oration for Scipio to have delivered before a battle, for instance, or advice to Sulla on whether to retire from public office or not. Style was important, and delivery was crucial; it demanded intelligence to understand the details of the situation under scrutiny, the imagination to empathise with another man's feelings, the talent to coin the ringing phrase and the persuasive argument, the memory to learn all this by heart (reading from scripts was a sign of weakness) and above all the confidence to stand up and speak clearly in front of one's critics. The purpose of this education was obvious: if the boy went on to become a leader of troops then his powers of understanding and public speaking would be tested in front of his men, if he became a barrister then he would need these skills every day of his working life, and if he became a politician he would need to be able to persuade his fellow citizens to follow his advice. Many of the most important Romans in the late republic combined two of these three occupations (Cicero was barrister and politician, Marius, Pompey, Caesar and many others were generals and politicians) and any boy who had ambitions in the state had better learn the art of rhetoric first.

Secondly, education involved learning Greek. This was the language of culture and sophistication in the Roman world for a lot of people, and one sees (for instance) Cicero slipping into Greek quite naturally in his private correspondence.[3] The evidence suggests that many of the people who provided high culture and the 'life of luxury' in Rome were Greek[4] and that knowledge of this language was *de rigueur* for anyone who aspired to eminence.

Thirdly, literature itself was a vital part of education. We can see from the poetry itself that references there abound to Greek and Roman literature of the past and the present; he alludes to Homer, Tragedy, Comedy, Lyric and even didactic epic in his work. He seems to have been familiar with the work of his near-contemporary

Lucretius, and also had the knowledge of Greek required to translate whole poems by Sappho (51) and Callimachus (66) into elegant Latin verse. His use of mythology (such as the tale of Protesilaus and Laudamia in poem 68) is exquisite and looks forward to the poetry of Propertius a generation later; while his scathing social satire (such as poem 67) ranks him with the greatest satirists of Roman literature. Let us finish this chapter with just one poem to see how the issues raised so far can be used in reading Catullus.

Poem 30 is a fascinating text:

> Alfene immemor atque unanimis false sodalibus,
> iam te nil miseret, dure, tui dulcis amiculi?
> iam me prodere, iam non dubitas fallere, perfide?
> nunc facta impia fallacum hominum caelicolis placent,
> quos tu neglegis ac me miserum deseris in malis?
> eheu quid faciant, dic, homines cuiue habeant fidem?
> certe tute iubebas animam tradere, inique, me
> inducens in amorem, quasi tuta omnia mi forent.
> idem nunc retrahis te ac tua dicta omnia factaque
> uentos irrita ferre ac nebulas aereas sinis.
> si tu oblitus es, at di meminerunt, meminit Fides,
> quae te ut paeniteat postmodo facti faciet tui.

Alfenus, you are thoughtless and treacherous to your loyal friends. Do you feel no pity now, you hard-hearted man, for your sweet friend? Have you no hesitation in betraying me now, nor in deceiving me now, you traitor? Do the gods who live in heaven approve of the wicked deeds of liars now – gods whom you ignore as you abandon me, unhappy in my misfortune?

What are men to do, tell me, whom are they to trust? You certainly kept telling me to surrender my soul, you wicked man, leading me into your love as if all were safe for me. Now, despite that, you pull back and allow the winds and the clouds of the air to carry off all your words and deeds making them useless. Even if you have forgotten, the gods still remember, Honesty remembers; she will later on make you repent of your action.

Who is this Varus? A certain Alfenus Varus appears in poem 10 where his 'little tart' of a girlfriend succeeded in showing up the poet's eagerness to impress her; and there was a lawyer of that name in Rome at the time, as we shall see. The addressee's offence is vaguely hinted at but hardly spelled out: he had told the poet to 'surrender his 'soul' and 'led him into love'. Did this mean that he had introduced the poet to a third party who had gone on to betray the poet (with Varus himself?) Or is it merely expressing disappointment that the love / friendship between poet and Varus had been let down by an unspecified act of infidelity on the part of the latter? Certainly the word *fides* is given prominence and this all suggests a lack of trust emerging between poet and addressee.

Poems are not real life, however. If the poet does not specify the offence then presumably that is either because all his readers would know what it was and did not need telling, or else because the offence was too embarrassing to the poet to be mentioned; or thirdly and most probably because it does not matter and may not even exist. After all, poets have to write about something and it may be here that the poem is tailored to impress and move the audience and its addressee more for its form and style than for its content. There is certainly plenty to admire in the poetry: the juxtaposition of *facti faciet* in the last line, framed as that line is between *te* and *tui*; the variation of vocabulary whereby the poet keeps finding new ways to express the man's cheating (*immemor ... false ... prodere ... fallere ... perfide ... impia ... inique*); the lovely metaphor of the winds and the clouds of the air carrying off his words (a metaphor adopted later by Virgil, *Aeneid* 9.312–13). The rhetoric of the piece is excessive and possibly a mockery of the kind of plaintive oratory used then as now by lawyers to arouse sympathy: look for instance at how Cicero at about the same period excites our compassion for the hapless Cluentia whose husband was seduced by her own mother Sassia:

> The daughter, pained by the sort of suffering which any woman would feel and unable to bear the rivalry of her mother ... wanted others to be kept in the dark about her troubles, great as they were. In the hands and the embrace of this her most affectionate brother she grew old with grief and with tears ... O unbelievable wickedness of the woman! Unbridled and uncontrolled lust! Unparalleled audacity! She had no fear of the power of the gods and the opinion of men, nor of the very walls which had been witness to her earlier marriage ... (Cicero, *Pro Cluentio* 5.13–6.15)

'The power of the gods ... :' look again at the Catullus poem and ask why he uses the poetic and archaic word *caelicolis* (literally 'heaven dwellers') for 'gods' and why does he invoke them at all? Does this prayer express piety? Or desperation on the part of the poet? The links of the gods with human values is spelled out towards the end of the poem where we are told that 'the gods remember, and *Fides* remembers'. It is often said that any abstract noun was a Roman god if it had a capital letter on the front of it, and here the poet personifies Fides as a deity in her own right. Yet there is abundant evidence[5] that Romans doubted whether the gods cared too much about our moral lapses and such pleas as this smack of pain and despair more than any certainty about the reliability of the gods.

The poet's stress on the word *fides* (trust, faithfulness) is revealing of a world where evidence of a man's words or actions was limited and so sanctions had to be imposed to be sure that his word could be believed; the language of line 6 ('tell me, what are men to do and whom are they to trust?') suggests that human society can only function in a system of oaths which can be relied upon – promises and actions which Alfenus has now retracted. Of course the word *fides* has a whole range of meanings in politics and finance which may or not be relevant to the meaning of this poem – it denotes credit-rating in financial circles, a guarantee of immunity from prosecution in diplomacy, as well as the more immediate 'trustworthiness' in common parlance. All of this may well have been the language which Alfenus was familiar with and used in his daily work; what is intriguing here is how the term is used to denote a highly emotional scenario ('surrendering my soul') rather than the hard world of politics and high finance. Similarly the word *amicus* (usually translated 'friend') denotes a political running mate and so here again we see the poet adopting the language of political alliance for a very unpolitical scene, the gap being stressed by the diminutive form of the word (*amiculi*), itself strengthened by the qualifying term 'sweet' (*dulcis*) with the implication that it had been used by Alfenus to the poet at some time and was here being thrown back at him.

One further consideration in reading this poem is of course the metre in which it is composed; the poet chose the difficult and unusual 'Greater Asclepiad' metre for this text (a metre he uses for no other poem in the collection) and the rhythm alone sets it on a higher register of solemnity than would be the case with other metres. The poem is composed in lines of 16 syllables, whose rhythm is:

– – – UU – / – UU – / – UU – U x

quos tu neglegis ac me miserum deseris in malis

This was the metre in which the third book of the poems of Sappho was composed, a book of which nothing survives; and if nothing else this reinforces the case for regarding Sappho as in many ways an inspiring model for Catullus. What is easier to establish is that when Horace published his *Odes* in 23 BCE he composed one (1.18) to a certain Publius Alfenus Varus who seems likely to be the same as the addressee here, a man by now aged but still the formidable lawyer whom Catullus had teased in emotive language in this poem – and a man for whom (according to Horace) *fides* is still a problem. The name was unusual and his origins were (like Catullus') in Transpadane Gaul, which helps to place the addressee of Catullus' poem in the world of Roman lawcourts, a world where one's word had to be relied on under oath but where the good barrister would spin the facts to suit his client. For this person to be found wanting by Catullus for his lack of *fides* is highly charged and appropriate if the subject is a lawyer. For him to be upbraided in language reminiscent of the passionate speeches of the courts is of course doubly appropriate; the abandoned poet is not praying for but predicting the demise of his opponent with certainty and clarity and he is heaping the terms of abuse on the head of his victim with Ciceronian abundance.

To sum up, this poem reads in some places like a plaintiff in court pleading that his opponent has broken a contract with him with all the usual appeals to both the gods and to the practical problems which would arise for society if we allowed this sort of thing to go unpunished. Alfenus was no half-hearted participant, either: the strong word *iubebas* (you ordered) is picked up by the wheedling and mendacious reassurance that 'everything is now safe'. The poem works, in other words, better because we do not know what if anything lies behind it; this forces us to look at it for what it is, a piece of poetry and a study in style and language tailored to the recipient and no more to be taken at face value than the lyrics of a song. The text can be enjoyed on its own terms exactly for what it is: a wonderfully skilful example of metrical and linguistic ingenuity, adopting a posture of aggrieved honesty in the face of treachery. It may reflect something or nothing in 'real life'; but what it certainly reflects is the sensibility of the educated poet to create literature out of the tradition of the poets of the past but also with a voice which the Romans of his day would respond to. That Catullus moved in distinguished circles is suggested by this poem to a distinguished man: that he expected his poems to be enjoyed in those circles is also suggested by the sophistication of this text.

CHAPTER 2

THE POET AT WORK

Catullus has often been seen as the bringer – or at least one of the collaborators – of a revolution in Roman poetry – a very influential book by Kenneth Quinn in 1959 was simply called *The Catullan Revolution*. This image of Catullus and his friends blazing a new trail in the tired old world of Roman poetry is of course drawn from the self-promoting claims of Catullus himself and is hard to assess fully because so little of the earlier poetry survives. There is, however, plenty of evidence that much of the earlier literature was less tired (and more similar to Catullus' own) than he would have cared to admit – but none of this is to denigrate from the achievement of this most popular of all Roman poets. After the epics of earlier poets with their grand accounts of earlier history, Catullus and his friends spring out of the pages of his own poetry and allow us to see the poet writing poems which are a response to other poems – and they seem to have formed something of a coterie of poets whom Cicero somewhat scathingly referred to in Greek as 'The Newer Men' (*Neoteroi*) – from which is derived the term 'Neoteric' which is often used to describe the poetry of Catullus and his circle. Cicero also referred to them as *cantores Euphorionis* or 'singers of Euphorion'. But who was Euphorion? What relation did he have to the poetry of Catullus? This chapter is going to look at the style and the school of writing which Catullus has come to represent and which accounts for his place in Roman literature.

Here is the poet at play:

> Yesterday, Licinius, with time on our hands,
> we played around on my writing tablets a lot
> as we had agreed to play at being intellectuals,
> each of us writing little verses
> playing now with this metre, now with that,
> answering each other's ideas over jokes and wine.
> I came away from there on fire with your
> elegance, Licinius, and your humour,
> so that neither food was any use to me in my wretched
>   state
> nor would sleep cover my little eyes with rest,
> but wild with frenzy I tossed all over the bed
> longing to see the dawn,
> to speak with you and be with you.
> But after my limbs were lying half-dead
> exhausted with toil on the little bed,
> I made this poem for you, my dear man,
> so you could see my agony.
> Now do not be rash. I beg you
> do not spit back our prayers, apple of my eye,
> in case Nemesis demands punishment from you.
> She is a powerful goddess; beware of injuring her.
>   Poem 50

The Licinius in question is almost certainly Caius Licinius Calvus Macer (82–47 BCE), the author of a short epic poem *Io*. This poem shows the poet using poetry as a fun thing to do with other poets – almost like a game of scrabble. The keyword 'at leisure' (*otiosi*) marks the poetry as entertainment rather than serious moral or didactic literature. The essential features of the poetry whose composition is here being described – and the poem before our eyes for that matter – are wit, humour, elegance rather than anything solemn or serious. There is a sexual undertone to the poem too, but this is not (I think) to be pressed too hard. The word he uses for 'playing' (*lusimus*) was also used of young men 'playing the field' and sowing wild oats: and the description of the night-time insomnia of the poet reminds us of the lover similarly racked with insomnia: and lastly the poet addresses Licinius with the term *ocelle* (literally meaning 'my little eye') which is elsewhere used of a lover. That this is not to be taken at face value is shown by the way in which Catullus also addresses the town of Sirmio as *ocelle* in poem 31, and also by the way in which the poem makes use of the hymn formula as often used in addressing gods; first the poet reminds Licinius of what he has done in the past (as if Licinius needed telling what he had done the day before) before going on to make his prayer. The mock-religious invocation of Nemesis at the end makes this note more obvious. There is at first sight little odd about poets writing of their own composition methods; Catullus' contemporary Lucretius speaks several times of the 'sweet labour' of poetry writing, also mentioning that he dreams of writing poetry (4.969–72) but a passage in book 1 of the *de rerum natura* (1.140–5) is closer to Catullus here:

> Your merits and the hoped-for pleasure of your sweet friendship urges me to carry out any amount of effort and gets me to spend the quiet nights awake, trying to find the words and the poetry with which I could finally be able to convey clarity and light to your mind, to let you see into the heart of hidden things.

The passage quoted shows a link between poetry and friendship and the poet's urge to seal the friendship with the poetry: but Lucretius was writing for Memmius who was not a philosopher (though he did write poems) and his purpose is to illuminate the thinking being expounded; Catullus is here relaying a mutual passion for composition. Catullus' language is also closer to the Greek concept of poetic madness than to Lucretius' cool enjoyment of judicious wording. Put very simply, the Greek concept of poetic inspiration runs something like this. You sit down and look at a blank sheet of paper, with nothing on the paper or in your head; an hour or two later the paper is full of poetry. Where did it come from? It did not exist before the session and so it must have been given by the gods – and so the idea of the Muses came into being. Plato pokes gentle fun at his rhapsode Ion who claims possession by the god when he is declaiming Homer (Plato, *Ion* 533e3–534a5) but there were many who saw the creative act as being one of divine madness (*theia mania*: Aristotle, *Poetics* 1455a; Horace, *Ars Poetica* 300, 453–76). Catullus here uses the same idea to hyperbolic effect, in that the passion is spelt out large but the genre of poetry being produced is light and almost trivial.

So this text tells us a lot more about Catullus and his friends than we at first thought. In the first place the composition of poetry can be a fun thing to do and it bears more than a passing resemblance to love. Love, as we shall see in the next chapter, was often seen as something to be indulged in one's spare time so long as it did not interfere with the man's duty and work; similarly here, the faint madness of the poet is not a million miles away from the madness of the lover who is also racked by insomnia to the point where he acknowledges the absurdity of his situation (e.g. Horace, *Odes* 4.1). Given that a lot of Catullus' poems are love poems and many of them express his own particular brand of recalcitrant madness for a lover (e.g. poem 8, 76) this poem shows the lighter side of his obsessiveness. More interestingly, the language of the poem is clearly hyperbolic – the failure to eat and sleep, being 'wild with madness', limbs being 'half-dead', the reference to the spirit of righteous indignation Nemesis – and this all points to the ironic nature of the poem being composed. In other words, it is hard to

take the words at anything like face value and it is as if the whole
text is contained in inverted commas; a sophisticated exercise
in expressing an unsophisticated passion, a poem about 'playing'
which is itself playful in its invocation of a god. It praises Calvus
but also shows Catullus as being a worthy companion and equal to
him in wit and poetic grace.

For another example of poetic irony at work see the next poem
in the collection. This poem is mostly a translation of a poem by the
early Greek lyric poetess Sappho, but it ends with an odd stanza – a
stanza which is so apparently odd (and not in the Sappho original)
that some scholars regard it as not belonging to this poem at all but
being a fragment of a different poem altogether. Here is the poem:

> That man seems to be to be equal to a god,
>   that man, if it is right to say so, seems to me to outdo the
>   gods;
> the one who, sitting opposite you again and again
> sees you and hears you
> laughing sweetly – a thing which steals
> all my senses, love-sick as I am. From the moment
> I caught sight of you, Lesbia, I have no voice left
> in my mouth
> but my tongue is sluggish, a slender flame
> steals under my limbs, my ears ring
> with their own sound, my twin eyes
> are covered with night.
>
> **************
>
> Idleness, Catullus, is a nuisance to you:
> you exult and get too excited in idleness;
> idleness has destroyed kings in the past
> and prosperous cities.
>
>   Poem 51

The first three stanzas are clearly a love poem of some sort, but the last stanza seems to be a personal reflection by the poet on his own state of mind – somewhat in the manner of poem 8 or poem 76. It is as if the poet were saying to himself: 'that's enough of all this romantic Greek stuff' or as if he were distancing himself from the very declaration of love, which the poem purports to contain. It certainly makes it harder to accept the old biographical notion that this poem was the first poem which the poet sent to the married lover whom he calls Lesbia – she could (the theory goes) pass this off as a mere translation if her husband found it. Such a theory may well be true but its error is that it substitutes history for literary criticism and assumes that explaining a biographical 'use' of a text is somehow relevant to a discussion of its quality as literature. The question of whether it was ever 'used' in this way is interesting but ultimately irrelevant; what is fascinating to the critic is the literary conundrum thrown up by a poem which appears to demonstrate a mastery of poetic technique while also calling into question its value. The 'leisure' which is vilified in the final lines is the same poetic *otium* in which Virgil sees himself composing his great poem the *Georgics* (4.563–5; 'flourishing in the pursuits of inglorious leisure') or which Ovid describes as being the poet's alternative to getting a real job in the real world (*Tristia* 4.10.17–40). It was *otium* which allowed Catullus and his friend Licinius to compose their verses together in poem 50, and the link between *otium* and poetry is thus one of strong interdependence.

So the last stanza of the poem has a self-deprecating touch – 'you have too much time on your hands, Catullus'. It ends, however, with a moralising generalisation of no obvious relevance to the poem or the poet – a 'political' reason to justify a personal statement. If lines 13–14 cast doubt on the love poetry of lines 1–12, then the last two lines of the poem cast ironic doubt on the doubt itself with a parody of the sort of sententious moralising which might be expressed by the puritanical old men he mocks in poem 5. We are at the end left none the wiser – but we are left with a poem whose meaning cannot be reduced to a state of love, a controlled account of a loss of control, a sophisticated account of a state of unsophisticated passion. The form and the content make up a mismatch which point to the artificial nature of the text and the skill of the poet in using words to recreate feelings and moods.

Getting back to Licinius and Catullus, then, we can now begin to see the sort of poetry which they were writing. Other poets enter the frame as we read the text: the poet's friend Cinna – the probable source for Cinna the poet in Shakespeare's *Julius Caesar* – produced a short epic called *Zmyrna* after nine years of hard work polishing it up, while the epic poet Hortensius has (allegedly) written five hundred thousand lines in that time. *Zmyrna* will be read for ages to come while the *Annals* of Volusius will soon be used to wrap fish.

> The *Zmyrna* of my friend Cinna has been published at last, after nine
> harvests and after the ninth winter after it was begun,
> while all the time Hortensius ... five hundred thousand in
> one ... (*gaps in text here*)
> ...
> *Zmyrna* will be sent all the way to the holy waves of the
> Satrachus;
> hoary ages will long read *Zmyrna*.
> But the *Annals* of Volusius will die right at the Po
> · and will often provide loose wrapping for mackerel.
> May my friend's small-scale monument be dear to my
> heart;
> And let the people rejoice at the inflated Antimachus.
> Poem 95

These *Annals* of Volusius are elsewhere mocked in Catullus as being 'paper full of crap' (36.1), while Antimachus had composed long (and popular) epic poetry in Greece 400 years before Catullus' own day. The contrast of the slender elegant miniature epic (which will travel far and live long) with the flatulent epic of lesser poets (which will get no further than the local river and end up wrapping mackerel) is made explicit in this poem. Interestingly, the poem also contrasts the new poetry with Greek poetry of several centuries before: Antimachus, whose poem *Lyde* was described by Callimachus (fr. 398Pf) as 'fat and inelegant' is said by Catullus to be 'swollen' (*tumido*). The critical discriminator seems to be one of quality over quantity. Neither Volusius nor Cinna's works have survived in fact, but the rate of composition could hardly be more different; a short epic of (say) 500 lines contrasted with half a million lines means that Hortensius was producing a thousand lines for every single one of Cinna. More means worse and small is beautiful – this seems to be the poetic manifesto of the friends of Catullus. The final line of this poem also shows a sense that real poetic worth will be lost on the masses who seem to enjoy 'blockbuster' epics rather than the perfectly formed miniatures of a Cinna, a Calvus or a Catullus – the sort of literary snobbishness born of frustration which Martin Amis explores in his recent novel *The Information*, or which Truman Capote well captured in his jibe at the works of Jack Kerouac: 'it isn't writing at all, it's typing'.

This elevation of the small form was not new to Catullus and his friends. It is time to meet the Alexandrian poets and look at the evidence for who exactly Cicero meant by the 'Neoterics'.

The Egyptian city of Alexandria (founded by Alexander the Great) was, in the time of Catullus, one of the greatest cities in the world. In the period from 280 to 240 BCE, as the cultural centre of the Greeks, Alexandria was the birthplace of some of the greatest literature produced in the ancient world. Poets such as Callimachus, Theocritus, Apollonius Rhodius and the Euphorion to whom Cicero was referring in his description of the New Poets as 'Singers of Euphorion' – all these reacted to the literature which preceded them and determined to be more than mere derivative epigones: and it was their poetics and their example which still lived and breathed in the poetry of the so-called Neoterics in Rome two centuries later.

Reading Alexandrian literature is not always easy. These writers expected their readers to have a wide vocabulary and an even wider range of background knowledge with which to understand their works. The techniques of allusion to other literature and sometimes recondite periphrases to denote people and places suggests that this was literature meant for *literati*, not for the man in the street. Finally, the Alexandrian writers appear to have cultivated an aesthetic of 'art for art's sake' which was in conscious reaction against the didacticism of earlier poetry, whose usefulness was traditionally accounted for in terms of the good advice or moral instruction it provided. Paradoxically, the Alexandrians produced the most thoroughly didactic poets of all – Nicander of Colophon's didactic epics on *Venomous Reptiles* and *Antidotes to Poisons* for instance – but the studied didacticism of these works fooled nobody. They were hardly manuals for the hill walker, but ingenious and artistic exercises designed to show off the skill of the poet in his ability to transform anything into refined verse. No longer did the poet concern himself with 'high' style and 'high' society, telling great tales of kings and heroes, either: the Alexandrians show a keen interest in the feelings and the everyday lives of 'ordinary' people. Alexandrian poetry gave its readers a new angle on old legends, the delightful detail rather than the thunder of grandeur, the artistic word order and exquisite euphony which repays repeated readings, the arch periphrases and allusions, the refusal to employ a straight linear narrative and the complex symmetry of construction.

So who were the poets whom we call 'neoterics'? We only have the term 'Newer Poets' from a critical remark of Cicero; in 50 BCE, Cicero wrote to Atticus (*ad Att.* 7.2.1) 'We came to Brundisium on the 24th November after having your special luck in seafaring – so fair for me

flauit ab Epiro lenissimus Onchesmites

('blew from Epirus the gentlest Onchesmites'). That verse with its spondaic ending you could pass off as yours or any of the "newer poets" you like'.

The word Cicero uses for 'new poets' is Greek, and the word he uses for 'spondaic' is also in Greek: this immediately suggests that the poets referred to used Greek terminology and Greek literary ideas in their writing. When we look at the line which Cicero composed, it displays the following features which (again) we can ascribe to the poets he is parodying: it is a line of hexameter verse (the metre used for epics both great and small) and it has an unusual spondaic fifth foot where both syllables are heavy: the final two feet are entirely occupied by a single four-syllable word – in fact the entire line consists of only four words (counting *ab-Epiro* as a single item). There is the choice of vocabulary, with Onchesmus in Epirus being used to coin a word (only found here) to denote a breeze from that south-western part of Epirus, a coinage which relies on the reader's knowledge to make the line make sense: there is the gentle alliteration of the letter *s* to support the blowing of the breeze. It is as good a line as many which we find in the extant remains of the New Poets, and it is hardly surprising that Cicero (who wrote poetry himself) was quietly proud of it. If we examine the text of Catullus we find similar features to the ones which Cicero produced: the fifth-foot spondee (76.15, 64.3), the learned reference (95.5), the line created out of a very few words (6.11, 38.8, 100.1), the long proper name to conclude a line (116.2, 66.66), and so on.

The group of poets around Catullus of whom we know the names were: Calvus, Cinna, Cato and Cornificius, and sadly only fragments of their works remain. That they formed a poetic 'school' is open to doubt but they certainly seemed to have composed a similar range of poetry: epigrams, wedding songs, occasional verse in a variety of metres with erotic, obscene, humorous or satirical content. The poetic form most obviously favoured by these poets was the short epic or *epyllion* such as poem 64 of Catullus or the *Zmyrna* of Cinna, the *Io* of Calvus, the *Glaucus* of Cornificius, the *Diana* of Valerius Cato, the *Dindymi Domina* of Caecilius (mentioned in poem 35): this sort of poem was minutely crafted in form (the *Zmyrna* took nine years to write, according to Catullus (95.1–2)) and would aim and claim to be original in content – looking at a familiar story from an unfamiliar viewpoint, as had been done in Callimachus' *Hecale*, or switching to another story by means of an *ecphrasis* – the *ecphrasis* was a digression whereby the main narrative pauses while the poet describes a work of art or a landscape and this often led to a story within a story as in the Theseus and Ariadne episode in Catullus' short epic poem 64. The subject matter was often love, especially 'pathological' love such as that of a girl for her father (*Zmyrna*) or of a mortal for a sea nymph (Catullus 64), or of a merman sea god who fell for the nymph Scylla (*Glaucus*), or the mysterious world of Cybele as expounded in Caecilius' *Dindymi Domina* (and by Catullus in poem 63), all the sort of stories which could be found in the Greek poet Parthenius' *erotica pathemata*, a work with a great influence on poets of this generation. The interest in pathological love which we find in these short epics is mirrored also in the pathological love which we also find in the short poems where the poet expresses the sort of feelings which elsewhere (e.g. 64.132–201) are put into the mouths of mythological heroines and heroes.

The short epic does not aim to tell the whole story, but rather expects the reader to know the whole story and to be able to appreciate the artistry of the poet who has sculpted what appears to be a miniature fragment of it in such unfragmentary perfection. This leads us on to another major Alexandrian feature: learning (*doctrina*). Alexandrian literature demands knowledge of history, geography and mythology and teases and flatters the reader with its arch allusive style: Catullus, who was later termed *doctus* by Martial (1.61.1, 14.100) and Ovid (*Amores* 3.9.63), alludes to such things as literary history (e.g. *Battiades* 116.2), geography (4.6–15, 7.4, 11.5–12), mythology (e.g. *Thyonianus* in 27.7). More striking still is the poet's use of contrasting binary themes (faithful friends vs unfaithful woman, for instance, in poem 11) and his interest in the bizarre (poem 90), the obscure (poem 66), the unexpected (the shifts of feeling and perspective in poem 8, the self-mockery in poem 10), and the aesthetic concentration on the poems as things in themselves which can wound (12.10–11, 40.2) or bless with immortality (6.16–17) or curse with notoriety (poem 40) and whose creation can render the poet sleepless with excitement (poem 50) and the reader mad with lust (poem 35). It is worth lingering over the poems in which Catullus speaks of poetry itself to develop a picture of his notion of the importance of poetry and of the interaction with other poets.

Many literary 'groups' define themselves negatively by contrasting their own practice with that of other (inferior) writers, as Callimachus famously did in his influential preface to the *Aitia*. Catullus defines the 'good poetry' of himself and his friends primarily by contrast to the 'poor poetry' of long-winded, bombastic epic which (he claims, as Horace also claims later (*Satires* 1.4)) was turned out by the yard by inferior poets with no talent except stamina. We mentioned earlier how in poem 36 he calls the *Annals* of Volusius 'paper full of crap' and the contrast of their style is evinced in the Catullan style of prayer (36.11–15) with its learned religious references over against the poetry of Volusius which is (he says) 'full of the countryside'. Catullus is (at it were) showing off how he writes and also giving Volusius a free writing lesson. Suffenus is similarly derided in poem 22 for the elegant (and expensive) appearance of his book hiding the 'rustic' contents, which are prodigiously long: another waste of good money and paper (although the ending of this poem is interestingly modest and rather reduces the polemical tone). A parcel of such bad poetry is seen in poem 14 as deserving a counterblast both in the poem itself and in a return parcel of named bad poets. In poem 50 we saw the poet recalling a session of poetry writing with Calvus and the emphasis throughout is on the contrast between the 'lightness' and 'playfulness' of the verse and the very serious effects it had on the poet whose passionate response is one more appropriate to a lover. This sort of verse may be 'slender' and light, but that does not mean it is not to be taken seriously – quite the reverse, for all the poet's self-effacing talk of 'trifling efforts' in the first poem of the book (*nugas* 1.4). Poetry is called for when in a depressed state (poem 38) or is needed to punish the wrongdoer (poem 40). Poem 35 is a brilliant combination of the 'invitation' poem with praise of the poet's friend's success with the girls and also praise of his poetry: Caecilius is called a *poeta tener* ('love poet' a term applied later by Horace (*Ars Poetica* 333) to Propertius) who writes 'charmingly' (*uenuste*) – and so inspires love (of which Venus was the goddess) in his female readers. What this shows is that Greek poetry was very much still in constant circulation, and that Callimachus' estimation of the earlier poet Antimachus was being copied word for word by Catullus. This contrast of the elegant literature of a Callimachus and the boorish alternative is the note on which our collection ends, as Catullus expresses his determination to use the weapons of the mudslinger rather than throw pearls before swine. The book thus closes with a further affirmation of the Callimachean literary values of elegance, wit, grace, brevity and charm. We receive the impression that Catullus formed a bond of solidarity with other poets of like mind (*sodalis* 95.9) and they established a bond of hostility towards poets who did not share their Alexandrian love of the exquisite miniature.

Key words mark out the aesthetic landscape which Catullus and his fellow poets inhabit. Most Roman poets aspire to the Alexandrian quality of 'learning' (*doctrina*) and Catullus is no exception: but he also uses a range of aesthetic terms which are characteristic of his group. Terms such as *lepidus* ('delightful') and *venustus* ('lovely') occur twelve and eleven times respectively, *bellus* ('pretty') turns up fifteen times; these indicate a policy of *l'art pour l'art* rather than any didactic message – except, that is, for the didactic message about how one ought to write poetry. Wit and cleverness are vital: the poet praises *sal* ('salt', metaphor for 'wit') nine times and the term *facetus* ('clever') occurs six times, as the poetry strives to impress for its originality and humour as much as for its technique – note also the approving use of *novus* ('new') right at the start of the first poem. The opposites of these terms are heaped as insults on the heads of the poets and people who are not in the same circle – so *illepidus, invenustus, insulsus, infacetus* are all applied to people who cross the poet's path artistically (e.g. 22.14) or who offend for their stupidity (e.g. 17.12) or behaviour (10.32, 12.5). Constantly in the poems the polar opposition is drawn between the city and the country: good poets and clever people are *urbanus* (39.10) while the dolt and the blockhead is *rusticus* (e.g. 22.9–10, 36.19).

This poet distances himself and his work from the simple and blunt and lays claim to refinement and artistry, even when (as often) the obscene content of the text strikes many modern readers as more 'blunt' and crude than 'refined' and 'urbane'. As we will see in chapter five, this tradition of poetic obscenity goes back a long way to the early Greek poets of the seventh century BC, and we find poetry both personal and public (Old Comedy, for instance) using obscene words and concepts freely. The sexual world of the

Romans seems to have been markedly uninhibited in this respect and the expression of sexual and excremental humour certainly seems to have been unrestrained by the same taboos as apply to many modern societies. Some of the obscene language used in this text is threatening – the poet (or his subjects) bringing male sexual aggression to express anger and a desire to dominate their enemies, such as in poems 15, 16 and 28. Some of it imputes sexual impotence – or incompetence – to the poet's enemies so that they are cuckolded (e.g. poems 17, 78); and some of it accuses the enemy of engaging in scatological acts which both amuse and disgust the reader (e.g. poems 88, 98) or engaging in incest (poems 89–91) or passive homosexuality (poem 112). The 'unclean mouth' is a regular theme in these obscene poems (e.g. 80, 97), as is the use of obscenity to provide 'punchlines' with which to end poems (e.g. 56). The composition of erotic poetry was not something to be ashamed of – even Pliny indulges in this pastime (*Letters* 5.3.2) and names plenty of other Romans who shared his interest – but neither was it to be taken as evidence of a *louche* lifestyle. The discontinuity between the life and the letters and the witty use of obscenity, are nowhere more clearly mapped out than in poem 16:

> I will bugger you and fuck your mouths,
> Aurelius you gay and Furius you pervert,
> for you thought from the evidence of my little poems
> that I was lacking in decency because they are lacking in
>   'manliness'.
> The decent poet ought to be pure
> in his life, but his little poems need not be like that at all;
> the poems do at least have wit and charm
> even if they are a bit sexy, lack decency
> and can go some way towards giving people the urge –
> I do not mean boys but those hairy men

who cannot shift their stiff loins.
You, because you read my 'many thousands of
kisses,' do you think me lacking in manliness?
I shall bugger you and fuck your mouths.

Poetry and real life are not one and the same thing. Poets can and do write obscene verses without themselves being anything other than citizens of irreproachable integrity. They may or may not be drawing on experiences they have had but in any case the point is still valid, that the text must stand as its own justification. What Catullus is doing here is producing a poem which asserts its independence of the behaviour of its creator. It stands on its literary merits, and so does the poet who is not to be judged by any similarities between the text and his life.

Poem 11 is a good instance of the ways in which the neoteric poet creates work which is both learned and also passionate, thus showing the interplay of form and feeling, of invention and allusion.

Furi et Aureli, comites Catulli,
siue in extremos penetrabit Indos,
litus ut longe resonante Eoa
    tunditur unda,

siue in Hyrcanos Arabesue molles,
seu Sagas sagittiferosue Parthos,
siue quae septemgeminus colorat
    aequora Nilus,

siue trans altas gradietur Alpes,
Caesaris uisens monimenta magni,
Gallicum Rhenum horribiles quoque ulti –
    mosque Britannos,

omnia haec, quaecumque feret uoluntas
caelitum, temptare simul parati,
pauca nuntiate meae puellae
    non bona dicta.

cum suis uiuat ualeatque moechis,
quos simul complexa tenet trecentos,
nullum amans uere, sed identidem omnium
    ilia rumpens;

nec meum respectet, ut ante, amorem,
qui illius culpa cecidit uelut prati
ultimi flos, praetereunte postquam
    tactus aratro est.

Furius and Aurelius, companions of Catullus
whether he will venture into the furthest Indes
where the shore is beaten by the far-resounding Eastern
    wave,

or whether he will go to the Hyrcans or the effeminate
    Arabs
or the Sagae and the arrow-bearing Parthians,
or the waves which the seven-fold Nile
stains,

or whether he will cross the high Alps
seeing the memorials of great Caesar
the Gallic Rhine and the shaggy Britons
far away,

as you are prepared to attempt all this,
whatever the will of the heavenly ones will bring,
announce to my girl a few
unkind words.

Let her live and thrive with her lovers
whom she grips in her embrace three hundred at a time
loving none of them truly but again and again
breaking all their balls,

and let her not look back as she once did to my love
which has fallen thanks to her badness like a flower
at the edge of the meadow, after it has been touched
by the passing plough.

This is a fascinating poem. For one thing it is composed in Sapphics, like the love poem 51. For another thing the structure of the poem is clear; three stanzas addressed to the poet's friends and then three stanzas giving them the message for them to deliver to the poet's girl. The places named date the poem probably to the period after 55 BCE as it was then that Caesar crossed the Rhine and went to Britain, Gabinius went to Egypt and Crassus went to Parthia. This was the year when these places were in the news and so for the poet to mention all three military campaigns is surely more than mere coincidence.

Nor is it simply a poem about faithful male friends contrasted with unfaithful women, though it can be read like that. For one thing, his relationship with Furius and Aurelius is elsewhere described in far less honourable terms (see poems 15, 16, 21, 23–4, 26) and his sudden description of them as inseparable companions to the ends of the earth is possibly ironic in the extreme. What is the purpose served by them in this poem? They are male friend-figures ready to be loyal and steadfast to the poet in any adventure he cares to name, in contrast to the faithless woman to whom he has been faithful but from whom he has received no loyalty in return. The exotic adventures in the first three stanzas are described in exaggeratedly epic terms (note e.g. the compound adjectives 'arrow-bearing ... sevenfold' (*sagittiferos ... septemgeminus*), the Homeric-sounding 'far-resounding' and the glorious marching (*gradietur*) of 'great Caesar', although the poet harbours little respect in poem 93 for the great man); all this is perhaps in order to evoke a mood of shared masculine self-assertion (note the way he dismisses the 'effeminate' Arabs) with which he can dismiss his girl; the first three stanzas thus build up the voice without which he could not utter the following two stanzas, as he uses the bluntest of prose language to put the girl in her place in an attitude of indifferent dismissal.

Of course the language of the poem here is anything but indifferent. True indifference does not spell out the misbehaviour of the other person, let alone describe it in Sapphic stanzas. The penultimate stanza purports to be the poet's reason for dismissing 'his' girl; she can go and live with her three hundred (a Catullan way of saying 'countless' cf. poem 9.2) lovers; they are not respectable men but *moechis* ('adulterous males' cf. poem 94) and she embraces all three hundred at once (a bitterly comic exaggeration). Her insatiability is brought out by the word *identidem* ('again and again') as even three hundred men have to perform repeatedly to satisfy this woman.

The final stanza – like the ending of poem 8 – gives the lie to all this bluster, as the text ends on a note of pathetic sadness; after the self-assertion comes the true vulnerability, after the affected indifference comes the affection which can still express itself in the highly emotional language of the lover. The male who could stride across the Alps is shown at the end as a lover whose love can be destroyed simply by a touch, the callous brutality of the fourth and fifth stanzas is shown up in the deep sensitivity both of the content and of the style of the final stanza. The final simile which compares the poet's love to a flower touched by a passing plough is especially effective after the crude 'breaking their balls'.[6] The flower simile reminds the reader of Sappho's simile of the hyacinth trampled by herdsmen (fr.105c) and is thus appropriate to end this poem written in the Sapphic metre. It also recalls the theme of flower-plucking and defloration found in marriage hymns. The wedding song poem 62.39–47 for instance has this very point

> just as a flower grows hidden away in an enclosed
> > garden
> a stranger to the flock, torn by no plough,
> a flower which the breezes caress, the sun strengthens,
> > the showers bring out:
> many boys have desired that flower, as have many girls.
> The same flower, when it has shed its petals, plucked by a
> > slender fingernail,
> has been desired by no boys, nor any girls either.
> Thus it is with a girl: while she remains untouched, she is
> > dear to her people;
> When she has dirtied her body and lost the flower of her
> > purity,
> She remains neither welcome to boys nor dear to girls.

Catullus has again subverted the genres with his simile: traditionally the girl is the virginal little flower waiting chastely to be plucked by her husband, whereas here Catullus presents himself as the innocent flower while his girl is being plucked left right and centre by husbands who are unfortunately not her own.

Notice how fragile the love and the flower are if they can be killed with a mere touch. This brings out the power of the girl and the vulnerability of the man, but the simile is not totally apt to the context in that the plough did not intend to hurt the flower (it was merely going past it) whereas the poet's harm has been caused by her deliberate fault (*culpa*). The masculine world of the poet and his two male friends, the assertive dismissal of the girl with a harsh rebuke of studied indifference – all this melts into a final image of human hurt and poetic beauty. It is no accident that the simile was in turn imitated by Virgil in one of his most moving passages, where the dead body of the young warrior Euryalus is compared thus (*Aeneid* 9.435–7):

> Just as a crimson flower cut by the plough droops as it dies, or poppies with tired necks let their heads hang when they happen to be weighed down with rain.

Lesbia's Sparrow

Ancient readers all knew the sparrow of Lesbia. After the dedicatory poem 1 this short poem on the pet bird of the poet's mistress became as celebrated as any poem in the ancient world. It, with its companion poem 3, illustrates many of the poetic features of Catullus and his circle and also shows some of the problems and the pleasure to be encountered in reading this poetry. Poem 2 runs as follows

> passer, deliciae meae puellae,
> quicum ludere, quem in sinu tenere,
> cui primum digitum dare appetenti
> et acris solet incitare morsus,
> cum desiderio meo nitenti   5
> carum nescio quid lubet iocari
> credo, ut cum grauis acquiescet ardor   8
> sit solaciolum sui doloris,   7
> tecum ludere sicut ipsa posse
> et tristis animi leuare curas   10
> tam gratum est mihi quam ferunt puellae
> pernici aureolum fuisse malum,
> quod zonam soluit diu ligatam.

> (Sparrow, darling of my girl,

with whom she often plays and holds in her lap,
to whom she gives the tip of her finger as it pecks
and stir you to give her sharp bites,
when she is gleaming with longing for me
and wants to do some fooling about
so that when her heavy burning passion rests, I think
she can enjoy a little solace for her pain;
to be able to play with you, like the mistress,
and to raise up the sad passions of my heart,
is as welcome to me as (they say)
the little golden apple was to the fast girl
which undid her girdle which had been tied for a long
     time.)

The first thing which the reader notices here is the textual problem of the line numbering. The ordering of the lines in the manuscript of Catullus can be forced to make sense but many modern editors prefer the inversion of lines 7 and 8 as printed above. The detailed meaning of the poem is not immediately clear: is the sparrow imagined by the poet to be fortunate in enjoying the affection of the beloved, and so the poet is jealous of it? Or is the poet wishing that he too had something to play with and thus take his mind off his 'sad cares'? Is he mocking 'his girl' for being satisfied with a sparrow when he has so many cares? The poem is composed in hymnic formula in that it addresses the deity / sparrow and then describes it to itself before uttering the wish at the end. The style of animal poem was familiar from earlier Greek poets; and the mythical analogy at the end is fully in the spirit of this sort of 'learned' poetry. The myth is carefully chosen: Atalanta was as swift as she was beautiful and whoever wished to marry her had to beat her in a running race. Milanion cheated by throwing golden apples down to encourage her to stop to retrieve them and so his golden apples 'untied her virginal belt'. The male gets the sexual union he desires, just as Catullus desires sexual union with his girl. Unfortunately the union granted in the myth is only aspired to in the Catullus poem and we are left with a picture of a poet looking as if through a window at a scene of girl and sparrow enjoying the sort of playful harmony he can only long for.

The poetry becomes more arch and ironic in the lament when the sparrow dies in poem 3.

lugete, o Veneres Cupidinesque,
et quantum est hominum uenustiorum:
passer mortuus est meae puellae,
passer, deliciae meae puellae,
quem plus illa oculis suis amabat.
nam mellitus erat suamque norat
ipsam tam bene quam puella matrem,
nec sese a gremio illius mouebat,
sed circumsiliens modo huc modo illuc
ad solam dominam usque pipiabat.
qui nunc it per iter tenebricosum
illuc, unde negant redire quemquam.
at uobis male sit, malae tenebrae
Orci, quae omnia bella deuoratis:
tam bellum mihi passerem abstulistis
o factum male! o miselle passer!
tua nunc opera meae puellae
flendo turgiduli rubent ocelli.

Mourn, O Venuses and Cupids
and all you men of finer feeling!
The sparrow of my girl is dead
the sparrow darling of my girl
whom she loved more than her eyes;

for it was honey-sweet and knew its mistress
as well as a girl knows her mother,
nor would it move from that woman's lap
but hopping around, now this way and now that,
it would chirp constantly to the mistress alone.
Now it goes along a shady journey
that journey from which they say nobody returns.
Curses be upon you, evil shades
of Orcus, who eat up all pretty things.
so pretty is the sparrow you have stolen from me.
Evil doing, as, poor little sparrow,
through your efforts my girl's
little eyes are swollen and red with weeping.

Here the apparent sorrow is quickly rendered absurd by its inappropriate application to a bird. The poem follows the conventions of the funeral lament – invocation of the gods, description of the dead person, lament for the sorry state of the deceased. The poem enjoys its own rhetorical and stylistic force, especially in the description of the little bird treading its weary way down to the underworld, with sound effects such as *it per iter* with its repeated *it –e– iter* suggesting the footsteps of the bird; the long adjective *tenebricosum* ('dark, gloomy'), the stock phrase 'from which they say no man returns'. Lines 14 and 15 both end with a strong verb and both contain a part of the word *bellus* ('pretty') in imitation of the repetition found in laments. The poem sounds to us like burlesque parody of the dirge: and clearly the later Roman poet Ovid also found it funny to burlesque Catullus' sparrow into his own lament over the death of his girl's parrot (*Amores* 2.6). The poet ends his lament looking not at the dead bird but at his girl, who is now weeping and whose little eyes are red and swollen. Once again the poet foils our expectations – after a lament over the dead bird he ends with an almost cheeky remark that the grief has spoiled the looks of his girlfriend. As with poem 43 which purports to be a hate-poem towards Ameaena but ends up a love poem for Lesbia, so here the object of the poet's grief is not the little bird but the mistress who so laments his passing. And yet the poem still retains its charm in its description of the bird complete with the onomatopoeic verb *pipiabat* (chirped), with the comparison of the relationship between bird and girl as like that of a girl with her mother (so that the girl is mother to the bird) with its suggestion that while men may come and go this relationship was unique. The term *dominam* ('mistress') is nicely ambiguous – does he mean the bird's mistress or the poet's mistress? Then we realise that they are one and the same. The bird which was the rival or substitute for the poet in poem 2 is still in death the substitute for the poet. But in neither poem can we be sure of anything except the artistry of the poems and the skill of their creator.

Sirmio – there's no place like home

One of the loveliest parts of Lake Garda to this day is Sirmione with its 'house of Catullus' drawing in the tourists by the thousand. Catullus immortalised this place in one of his most attractive and accessible poems:

> Paene insularum, Sirmio, insularumque
> ocelle, quascumque in liquentibus stagnis
> marique uasto fert uterque Neptunus,
> quam te libenter quamque laetus inuiso,
> uix mi ipse credens Thuniam atque Bithunos
> liquisse campos et uidere te in tuto.
> o quid solutis est beatius curis,
> cum mens onus reponit, ac peregrino
> labore fessi uenimus larem ad nostrum,

desideratoque acquiescimus lecto?
hoc est quod unum est pro laboribus tantis.
salue, o uenusta Sirmio, atque ero gaude
gaudente, uosque, o Lydiae lacus undae,
ridete quidquid est domi cachinnorum.

Sirmio, little jewel of peninsulas and islands –
all the ones which either Neptune bears
in liquid pools and in the vast sea –
how gladly and how happily I see you,
scarcely believing that I have left Thynia and the Bithynian
fields and that I now see you in safety.
O what is more pleasant than to dissolve worries
when the mind lays down its burden and tired with
foreign toil we come to our own household
and rest in our familiar bed?
This is the one thing which makes up for such great toils.
Hail, o lovely Sirmio, and rejoice with your rejoicing master
and you, o waves of the Lydian lake
laugh all the guffaws you have at home!
Poem 31

The poem is clearly constructed around binary pairs of things – islands and peninsulas, lakes and seas, two Neptunes, Thynia and Bithynia, mind and body, home and bed. In the first line the name Sirmio stands central in between the nameless islands and peninsulas and the vocative *ocelle* ('little eye' 'jewel') is held over to the start of the next line. Eyes are very important in Catullus and many times he describes things he loves as being 'dearer to me than my eyes' (14.1, 82 etc). Sirmio is given an almost sexual charge by this word, emphasised as it is at the end of its phrase but at the start of a line. Sirmio is placed in the context of islands and peninsulas, and then the camera pans out to embrace all watery pools, on the vast sea, held by Neptune – both of him. The rhetorical repetition of *quam libenter quamque laetus* ('how gladly and how happily') combines variation of vocabulary (glad and happy) with alliterative repetition. The poet alludes to his time in Bithynia – presumably the time he describes in poem 10 as spent on the staff of the praetor Memmius – as *curis*, a word often used of the passions or cares of love, as in the famous opening line of the fourth book of Virgil's *Aeneid*:

At regina gravi iamdudum saucia cura

But the queen had now for a long time been wounded with a heavy passion

which adds to the sexual and emotional charge of the poem. Note here how he builds up the sense of foreign toil in the sequence of words *curis* ('cares') ... *onus* ('burden') ... *peregrine labore fessi* ('tired out with foreign toil'), only to cap it with the sublime ease of the following sequence of 'home' words: *larem ad nostrum* ('to our own household') *desideratoque acquiescimus lecto* ('we rest on our longed-for bed'). The mind 'drops its burden' in a metaphor of short power and a sequence of short words, before the protracted tedium of Bithynia is brought out with the long phrasing of *peregrino* ('foreign'). The poem ends with a learned allusion – the waves at Sirmio are Lydian because the Etruscans of that part of Italy were originally said to have come from Lydia – which is itself a joke in that the waves are therefore travellers (like the poet) who have come from East to West (like the poet) and so should laugh (with the poet). The use of 'laugh' to indicate pleasure and relaxation of toil and inhibition is paralleled in Greek (e.g. Aristophanes, *Clouds* 1078; Hesiod, *Theogony* 40) and here sums up the mood of the poem. The last few lines have effective repetition of *gaude / gaudente* ('rejoice / with (your master) rejoicing') and the last line is neatly framed with laughter words and also contains the dominant idea of 'home' in the word *domi*. Catullus has once again managed to bring off that poetic magic of composing a poem of great sophistication on the simplest of themes.

CHAPTER 3

THE LIFE OF LOVE

I hate and I love. Why I do that, you are asking perhaps?
I do not know. But I feel it and it is torment.
Poem 101

In the ancient world Catullus was more famous for his love poems, and one of them in particular, than for all the other poems in the collection. His famous poem immortalising his girlfriend's sparrow (discussed in the previous chapter) became in some ways his calling card. This chapter will look at the love poems of Catullus in the wider context of the sexual manners of the Roman world in which he lived.

The girl whom Catullus addressed directly in many of his love poems is called Lesbia by the poet. The ancient writer Apuleius tells us that this was a pseudonym – and most scholars have deduced that the 'real' woman was a certain Clodia Metelli, sister of the infamous tribune Publius Clodius Pulcher and the target of Cicero's speech on behalf of Marcus Caelius. Be that as it may – and the jury will always be out on the historical identification of this character in Catullus' poetry – it is interesting to see if the life of love as depicted and assumed in Catullus' texts is coherent and interesting for the light it sheds on the poetry.

It is often said that women in the ancient world were kept in a state of what was once called 'almost oriental seclusion'. Women never reached the legal status of adults and were not allowed to vote or hold office. They were kept in the possession of their father until marriage when they passed into the control of their husbands (although in the time of Catullus women were increasingly being married in a less formal manner which did not make them the property of their husbands). Virginity until marriage, monogamy – at least serial monogamy – afterwards, chastity enforced throughout. The role model for the ideal Roman woman is seen as Lucretia whose rape and suicide prompted the expulsion of the last of the early kings of Rome in 510 BCE; chaste, hospitable and industrious, still hard at work late at night sewing and directing the slaves, irresistible to the wicked Tarquin but well able to stand up to his mixture of pleas and threats:

> 'Be quiet, Lucretia' he said. 'I am Tarquin, I have a sword in my hand and you will die if you utter a sound.' The woman woke up terrified, She saw no help to hand and death facing her. Tarquin pleaded his love, pleaded with her, mixing threats with prayers ...
>
> Livy, *History of Rome* 1.58

She was only 'persuaded' by the threat of having her male slave killed and his naked corpse laid next to hers so that word would get out that she had been found in adulterous shame with a slave. But as soon as Tarquin had left she had to commit suicide out of shame even though her own behaviour had been blameless. This ideal of fragrant womanhood and iron fidelity to a husband might seem odd to put beside the apparently faithless and scandalous behaviour of some of the women who appear in Catullus. Let us look at one of the Lesbia poems with the chaste Lucretia still in mind:

> If there is any pleasure in recalling earlier acts of kindness
> thinking that one is a good man and has not
> violated solemn oaths nor misused the power of the gods

to deceive people in any contract at all,
then you have many joys waiting for you in your old age,
    Catullus
as a result of this thankless love of yours.
Whatever good words or deeds anyone can do for anyone
    else –
all these have been said and done by you,
for nothing, all of them invested in a thankless mind.
So why will you carry on torturing yourself any longer?
Why not harden your heart and bring yourself back to
    reason
and stop being lovesick when the gods are clearly not on
    your side?
It is difficult to lay down a long love affair suddenly.
Difficult, yes – but you have to do this somehow.
This is your one hope of safety, a battle you have to win,
you have to achieve this, possible or not.
O gods, if it is your job to take pity, or if ever
you have brought the last shred of help to someone on the
    point of death,
then consider my plight, lovesick as I am. If I have lived a
    decent life,
rid me of this disease and ruin which creeps like paralysis
through to the bottom of my limbs and has driven all joy
out of my heart. I am no longer asking for her to love me
    as I love her,
nor for her to be faithful – she is not capable of that
I want to be healthy, to cast off this foul disease.
Gods, give me this in return for the decency of my life.
        Poem 76

This poem is striking in many ways, even in translation. Love as

a disease, a sickness to be got rid of is something of a surprise
to all those readers of Valentine cards which assume that love is
wonderful and makes the world go round. For Catullus, love makes
the world stop in its tracks and he cannot function in his 'sick' state
of mind. This is not new in literature – Catullus himself (poem
51) had brilliantly translated the famous poem of Sappho which
itemises the physical symptoms of love ('I cannot speak, my tongue
is lethargic, a slender flame steals under my skin, my ears ring with
their own noise, my eyes grow dark') and anything which causes the
sufferer to lose sleep and appetite (as love famously does) deserves
to be seen by a doctor, one might think. But there is more to it than
this. Poem 76 is a reversal of the gender roles which the traditional
Roman family and most of Roman law enshrined. In Catullus' case
he is in the possession of the girl and not vice versa; his life is being
threatened by her bad behaviour and he is suffering almost as a
slave to his 'mistress' – a state for which the Romans coined the
term *servitium amoris* ('slavery of love'). Patriarchal societies should
not produce men like Catullus – men who find themselves bereft of
any means of protecting themselves except prayers to the gods (and
even his prayers are perhaps useless, as the qualifying remark 'if it is
your job to take pity ...' makes clear). Perhaps there is more to this
poem than meets the eye.

In fact the poem sets up something of a scenario in which the
persona of the speaker is the problem rather than the medium. He
addresses himself as 'Catullus' and seems to be inviting the reader to
look at himself as a third person. The 'justification' which he provides
for his claims of 'decency' are pretty bland – not committing perjury
or tricking people is hardly grounds for canonisation but both
bespeak forms of honesty which the girl is said to lack – and the
alleged job of the gods to provide last-minute help to those on their
deathbed is not appropriate for one who wishes to recover his health
and not lose his life. Death as a solution for unhappy love was always

available to the lover – as Ovid later was to remind us in his poem *Remedies for Love* (15–19) – and did not need divine assistance. There is then the studied and faintly ridiculous way in which the speaker motivates himself to be rid of the girl, his protestations that 'this is a battle that must be won' only serving to undermine his confidence rather than to express it. His stance is melodramatic, his prayers and protestations making him look more like the lovesick fool from Roman comedy than a person deserving of our admiration or even sympathy. His quasi-medical summary of the symptoms of this 'disease' are his attempt to control his condition, while his moral posture as the 'good citizen' at the start of the poem is his feeble attempt to bolster up the collapsed dignity of a failed lover. The last four lines spell it all out in hard plain terms. After all the rhetoric, the medical language and the prayers to disinterested gods we are left with a man in love with a woman who does not love him and who does not seem to care. The poem ends with a final prayer to the gods, but the logic of this has already been exploded earlier on. If gods do reward 'decency' and if Catullus has never put a foot wrong in his decent life, then why are the 'gods clearly not on your side'? Either the poet is lying about his decency or else the gods do *not* care about it. In any case, his examples of decent social living do not say anything about his behaviour in a sexual relationship – and his desperate need to use such public examples only underlines our suspicions of inadequacy in Catullus' personal life. So the poem ends with no reassurance from gods or (wo)men and no sense either that the poet emerges somehow morally victorious either. We see a sad picture of a man seeking to offset the humiliation of rejection with this pose of religious and moral rectitude. A similar picture of the sad lovesick poet emerges from poem 8:

> Wretched fool Catullus, stop acting like an idiot.
> Consider gone what you see to have died.

The sun used to shine bright for you once
when you used to come and go wherever your girl led you
a girl loved by me like no other girl will ever be loved.
At that time, when all those pleasures were going on
you wanted them and the girl did not say no –
then truly the sun shone brightly for you.
Now she does say no. You too, say no, you weakling!
Don't chase after a girl who is running away, don't live like
    a fool
toughen your mind up, put up with things, become firm.
Goodbye, girl – Catullus is now firm
he will not come looking for you nor asking you out if you
    don't want him.
You will be the one to suffer when nobody asks you out.
You bitch, what life have you got to look forward to?
Who will come near you? Who will think you are pretty?
Whom will you love? Whose girlfriend will you be said to
    be?
Who are you going to kiss? whose lips are you going to
    bite?
As for you, Catullus, be resolved. Stay firm.

Once again, as in poem 76, we see a study in sadness and repressed desire. The poem begins by addressing Catullus in the second person, then refers to himself in the first person ('me') and then refers to himself in the third person ('Catullus is now firm'). The poet sets up a persona in his own name and allows his audience to see his desperate attempt to express 'toughness' as being merely symptoms of his inner insecurity and desperation. For one think, if he really were 'firm' about his rejection of the girl then he would not be bothered to talk about her at all, let alone write poetry about her, a psychological point which he makes of 'Lesbia' elsewhere:

Lesbia abuses me a lot when her husband is around
and that idiot thinks this is wonderful.
You donkey, have you no sense? If she forgot me and kept
    quiet
then she would be free of love for me. As she snarls and
    nags
this shows that she not only remembers me but (more to
    the point)
she is angry. She is burning with feelings – that's why she
    speaks.
                    Poem 83

For another thing, his mocking catalogue of the sexual desert
which awaits her in later life only serves to show us his wistful
reminiscing on their own earlier sexual encounters – the poet breaks
off abruptly when he gets to 'biting the lips', not able to take the sex
any further in his mind if he is to 'stay firm' in his resolve to reject
her. The poet may be trying to discredit the girl, but she is clearly
winning on points.

   These poems may seem somewhat embarrassing for a Roman
poet to publish. They have to be seen side-by-side with the happy
love poems which also appear in the collection. Poem 5 for instance
has inspired many a more recent poem on the theme of 'gather ye
rosebuds while ye may'.

Let us live, my Lesbia, and let us love
and let us value the mutterings of puritanical old men as all
    worth
just one penny. The sun can set and rise again;
but when our short light has once set
it is one eternal night to be slept through.
Give me a thousand kisses, then a hundred.
Then another thousand, then a second hundred,

then at once another thousand, then a hundred.
Then, when we have many thousands of kisses
we will mess up the balance sheets, so we do not know the
    numbers
or so no bastard can give us the evil eye
when he knows that we have so many kisses.

In this poem the poet is forming a tiny conspiracy of two against the
forces of repression symbolised in the puritanical old men. For him,
living and loving are almost the same thing and the shortness of
the life means that there is no kissing time to be wasted, whatever
the older generation may mutter. This shows us a different way of
looking at love, and may lead now to a more general consideration
of the 'life of love' in ancient Rome.

Catullus poem 5 sets itself out as something of an act of rebellion,
after all. What was he rebelling against? Who is meant by the
'puritanical old men' and would they really know and care what this
young man got up to in his private life?

Our evidence on these issues is of course slight and partial.
Some features of the Roman life of love distinguish it from more
modern manners; there was little in the way of condemnation of
heterosexual activity in itself, but a lot of concern to protect the
virginity and therefore the reputation of unmarried daughters and
the fidelity of wives. No man, after all, wanted to bring up somebody
else's baby as his own and the horned cuckold was a figure of fun
throughout the Mediterranean world. Even in the relatively short
book of Catullus' poetry we find the nameless man in poem 17 who
lets his gorgeous wife play around and so deserves (says the poet)
to be thrown into the mud for his stupidity; in poem 67 a more
sensational case involves an impotent husband who has to get his
own father to deflower his bride for him. In both cases, the cuckold
and the impotent man is mocked as pathetic. Yet poem 68 sees the

poet describe an ecstatic sexual encounter with a married woman – so (it seems) the shame of adultery lay with the betrayed husband rather than the randy lover. Sexual experience was not hard to find for a young man who had money – apart from slave girls, who could be used for sexual purposes as for any other, there were foreign girls living and working in Rome. Some of them were what older books delicately term *demi-mondaines* and we would probably call them high-class escort girls. Girls who had conversation, musical ability, charm and sex appeal; girls who did not belong to a master or a husband and so who could choose if they wished to have sex with a man. The wife and slave had no choice about sleeping with their master and not sleeping with anyone else; these girls could say no and so their 'yes' meant an acceptance of the lover as a person rather than a mere fulfilling of a role. Romans could and did fall in love with girls such as this – who are to be found in many of the poems of Horace for instance – and one of the most striking attacks on love of this sort is to be found in the poetry of Catullus' contemporary Lucretius, who paints a vivid and sneering picture of the Roman *jeunesse dorée* obsessed with girls who are laughing at them behind their backs while spending all their money:

> 'Wealth vanishes and becomes Babylonian coverlets
> duty is neglected, their reputation grows sick and weak;
> perfumes and fine slippers from Sicyon laugh on his
>   mistress's feet
> and huge emeralds with their green gleam are encased in
>   gold ...
>   Lucretius 4.1123–7

These 'Venuses' as Lucretius calls them are shameless gold-diggers, who hide what he nicely calls the 'backstage' aspects of themselves and never show their true appearance to their lover. If he once saw them as they really are, Lucretius says, the lover would run for his

life. Now of course Lucretius has a philosophical and ethical axe
to grind here – his text is one which seeks to persuade the reader
to abandon the quest for romantic love, and so spare himself the
agony of unrequited love, in favour of a love which is easy to find
and readily available. So no exotic unavailable beauties when one
can buy a prostitute for relatively little money and at least see
what one is buying – a line of argument used later by Horace when
he pleads that in love one should not buy a pig in a poke (Horace,
Satires 1.2.101ff).

Many of the girls we find addressed in the personal lyrics of
Horace bear Greek names and it has been shown by Jasper Griffin
(*Latin Poets and Roman Life* ch. 1) that Rome at the time had a lot
of Greek men and women serving what one could call the 'life of
luxury'. Earlier generations of critics assumed that the Greek names
of Horace's girls meant that they showed that the poems were
elegant fictions based on Greek poetic forms and motifs; Griffin has
shown that this need not be the case. Catullus poem 45 shows us
a delightful picture of young love between a couple where the man
has a Roman name and the girl is Greek:

> Septimius holding his lover Acme
> on his lap, said 'My Acme,
> if I do not love you desperately and am ready to love you
> with total dedication for all the years to come,
> as much as any one who loves with desperation –
> then may I find myself alone in Libya and scorched India
> and come face to face with a green-eyed lion.'
> When he said this, Love, on the left as before
> on the right, sneezed approval.
> But Acme, bending her head gently back
> and kissing the swimming eyes of her sweet boy
> with her crimson mouth, said:

'So my little Septimius, my life,
let us be totally enslaved to this one lord
as a much greater fiercer fire
burns in the soft marrow of my bones.'
When she had said this, Love on the left as before
on the right, sneezed approval.
Starting out from favourable omens
they love and are loved with mutual feelings.
Love-sick little Septimius prefers Acme and Acme alone
to all your Syrias and Britains;
faithful Acme takes her delight and her pleasure
in Septimius and Septimius alone.
Who has ever seen people more fortunate?
Who has ever seen a more blessed case of love?

One thing which strikes the reader of this little idyll is the reference
to the boy preferring love to 'all your Syrias and Britains'. As in
Catullus 5, there is a slight stance of rebellion here – a sense that
society is expecting him to toe the military line and go off to
conquer far-off places and win military renown when all he wants is
to stay with his beloved instead. We get the feeling that the 'good'
Roman youth would – as Horace was later (*Odes* 3.2.1–4) to say – 'be
made tough by hard campaigns ... riding against fierce Parthians,
spreading terror with his sword' and not waste his time in love
affairs (and still less in writing about them). Sowing wild oats was
one thing, but living the life of the debauched libertine was quite
another. In a famous story (Horace, *Satires* 1.2.31–5 – though he
suppresses the punch line of the tale reported in later writers) the
stern Cato saw a young man leaving a brothel and congratulated
him for his good sense in satisfying his sexual urges in a socially
responsible way – the older man was less impressed on seeing the
same young man leaving the same brothel the next day as this

was spending too much time there. The figure of Mark Antony the libidinous lover of the Egyptian queen Cleopatra later came to stand for the irresponsible indulgence of the sex drive (though of course this was a travesty of the situation leading up to the battle of Actium) and the message seems to be that sexual affairs are fine so long as they are only hobbies, part of one's *otium* (leisure time) and not encroaching upon the vital *negotium* (business, duty) of the state or the regiment or the career. So love is seen as something to be indulged in parties, banquets, night-time assignations – but only so long as one is still able to function as the good citizen by day. How does this leave Septimius swooning over his Acme and prepared to forgo the conquests of East (Syria) and West (Britain)? Young though he seems to be ('little Septimius' might be an affectionate diminutive or might refer to his immaturity) he is still uttering a provocative gesture of defiance towards the Roman military machine. This theme of love versus soldiering takes two forms in later love poetry; on the one hand there is the repeated insistence that the lover chooses love over fighting for Rome – as in Propertius' famous lines (3.5.1–2)

> Love is a god of peace – we lovers worship peace;
>   I have enough tough battles with my mistress.

and on the other hand the theme that love is like warfare becomes the 'soldier of love' theme found in (e.g.) Ovid, *Amores* 1.9. Catullus does not go thus far – but it is interesting to see how seeds planted by him were to take flower in the work of later poets.

Catullus' poetry seems to suggest that he did in fact fulfil his role as a small part of the military outfit. Poem 10 shows the poet returning from his tour of duty on the staff of the governor of Bithynia and trying unsuccessfully to boast about his acquisitions there. Apart from this there are no references to any political activity on the part of the poet.

What is more surprising to a modern reader is the prevalence given to openly homosexual themes in Catullus' poetry. The young man Iuventius is singled out as the object of the poet's desire and 'my boy' is mentioned as somebody whom the poet wishes to keep for himself and not allow his friends to touch. Take poem 21 for instance:

> Aurelius, father of famines, past present and to come,
> you are randy to bugger my beloved boy.
> Nor do you keep your desires secret – you spend time with
>   him
> joking together, sticking to his side and trying all your
>   tricks on him.
> It's no good. You might lay traps against me
> but I will get you first by fucking your mouth.
> If you were doing all this with a full stomach I would keep
>   quiet about it;
> but I am angry that the boy will learn to starve and thirst
>   from you.
> So stop it, while you still may do so with modesty intact;
> or else you might stop it when you get your mouth fucked.

The 'mouth fucking' referred to is a powerful expression of control over another whereby the speaker forces the other man to give him oral sex. The joke here is that Aurelius' notorious meanness with food will be answered when the poet 'fills his mouth' with something other than food. The interest of the poem here is that Catullus appears to be protecting a young boy (*puer*) from the sexual desires of an older man and the tone of the poem is one of mock-jealousy rather than moral outrage against paedophilia. Poem 15 had asked (the same?) Aurelius to keep his hands (and his penis) from the poet's beloved boy;

> Move it (your penis) about where and how you like
> as much as you fancy and whenever you get the chance –
> I only ask for this one exception – and it's a modest request
>   I think (15.11–13)

The poet on this occasion threatens even more savage retribution if his wishes are not followed:

> with your feet pulled up and your door (i.e. anus) open
> radishes and mullets will run you through. (15.17–18)

Iuventius is addressed as 'little flower' and mildly rebuked for indulging the desires of Furius, while poem 99 shows the poet trying to pacify an outraged Iuventius who is angry that the poet has stolen a kiss from him. What is clear from that poem is that the younger man does not feel any desire for Catullus; he reacts to the poet's lips (99.10) 'as if it were the disgusting spit of some pissed-on tart' but the older man is devoured with longing for the boy. The language of poem 48 is oddly reminiscent of the heterosexual kisses of poem 5 quoted above:

> Iuventius, if someone were to allow me to carry on kissing
> those honeyed eyes of yours, then
> I would kiss them again and again up to 300,000;
> nor would I think I was ever going to have eaten enough,
> not even if the crop of our kissing
> were denser than the dry ears of corn.

and the telling word here is 'our' kissing which implies some feeling (real or perhaps imaginary) on the part of the boy. Desire for young boys seems to have been acceptable at least in some areas of society and the pattern seems to follow the Greek model, whereby the older male desired the younger and sought to impress him with his acts of courage and superior wisdom, while also disapproving of the youth if he granted his sexual favours freely. At no point was the boy expected to feel anything but perhaps respect for the older man. This differed completely from the disgust which many ancients felt for a homosexual love between two grown males and in particular for the one who played the woman's role in sex.

Catullus heaps ample abuse on these 'pathic' homosexuals. Poem 112 singles out a certain Naso:

> You're a great man, Naso, and there's not a great number of men who don't
> fuck you. Naso you're a great man and a pansy.

while poem 57 picks on the great Caesar himself:

> They make a good pair, the shameless perverts
> Mamurra and bumboy Caesar ...

Poem 33 alleges that Vibennius' son 'cannot sell his hairy buttocks for a penny'. All this suggests that the worst thing for a man to be called is a pathic, while the red-blooded male may well wish to penetrate attractive youths for pleasure or other men to show his superiority over them ('I will bugger you and fuck your mouths, Aurelius the pansy and Furius the pervert ...' 16.1–2). We may, however, be in danger of taking this metaphorical language too literally. When the poet uses this language to describe how he was 'done over' by his own boss Memmius in Bithynia:

> Memmius, well and long did you screw me slowly
> as I lay on my back, with that long beam of yours! (28.10–11)

we are no more inclined to take him at face value than when he referred to the same Memmius as an *irrumator* (one who forces others to give him oral sex) in poem 10.12. The language of abuse then as now commonly uses themes of sexual humiliation to express itself and there is no need to press the words more closely. This does not, however, reduce the Iuventius poems to mere stylish metaphors; and the evidence suggests that the open expression of desire of heterosexual men for young men as well as young women seems to have been far more widespread then that it is now. There is the suggestion in the wedding hymn poem 61 that the bridegroom should now abandon his catamite in favour of his wife:

> They say that you find it difficult,
> O perfumed bridegroom, to keep away from the smooth-
>   skinned boys
> but keep away from them. (61.133–5)

although (once again) one should beware of taking the sort of ribald mocking found in a modern best man's speech at face value.

Catullus is known for his love for Lesbia, but she was not the only girl to be named in his poems as a sexual partner. Ipsitilla for instance is addressed in quite unambiguous terms:

> Please, my sweet Ipsitilla,
> my darling, my charming girl,
> tell me to come to you after lunch
> and (if you give the word) help me by seeing
> that nobody bolts the street door
> and that you don't decide to go out,
> but rather stay at home and make ready for us
> nine consecutive fuckifications.
> If there's a chance, give me the word right away –
> for I am lying on my back, full of food
> banging through my cloak and tunic.
>   Poem 32

Nobody knows who this girl was – though it is at least possible that the name was a comic diminutive of *ipsa* (the mistress). All the sweet talking of the first couple of lines are clearly an attempt to get the 'fuckifications' which the poet really craves. A more sensitive picture of love emerges from one of the most impressive poems in the collection, poem 68.

In the context of a discussion of love in the poems of Catullus this poem is quite surprising and constantly elusive. The poet begins as an epistolary poem to a certain Allius describing the poet's misfortunes; his grief over his dead brother has robbed him of all his joy and his libido. This leads him to describe the way in which Allius assisted him in providing a house in which the poet and his mistress might make love. The love between them is compared to that of the legendary heroes Protesilaus and Laudamia – an ominous comparison as their short marriage was ended when Protesilaus went to the Trojan War and was killed – which links into the death of the poet's brother who also died in that part of the world. The meeting of the poet and his mistress (who is not named) is not described except in general terms and his lover's own infidelity is something the poet can shrug off:

> my darling brought herself into my embrace,
> with Cupid darting frequently around her, now here now
> there,
> shining brightly in his saffron tunic.
> She may not be content with Catullus alone,
> but we will put up with the infrequent infidelities of my
> modest mistress
> in case we turn like stupid men into bores ...
>
> she gave me stolen little gifts in the wondrous night time
> gifts taken right from the embrace of her own husband.
> (68.132–7, 145–6)

What is striking here is the way in which the poet both exults in his own 'theft' of another man's wife but also recognises that she is *ipse facto* an unfaithful woman and so no more likely to be faithful to Catullus than she is to her husband. Love for many Romans was something of a leisure-activity pastime, but this poem (like poem 5) suggests more than that. His girl is:

> far above all others, she who is dearer to me than I am to
> myself,
> my light, whose life makes living sweet. (68.159–160)

Here is the whole poem in translation:

> *You, ground down with misfortune and bitter bad luck,*
> *Still send me this letter written in tears,*
> *like a shipwrecked man thrown up from the foaming waves of*
> *the sea*
> *for me to rescue and bring back from the threshold of death;*
> *You, a man whom neither holy Venus allows to rest in soft*
> *sleep,*   5
> *abandoned on his bachelor bed,*
> *nor do the Muses delight you with the sweet song of writers of*
> *old,*
> *since your troubled mind can find no rest:*
> *this is welcome to me, since you call me your friend*
> *and you ask me for the gifts of the Muses and of Venus.*   10
> *In case you are unaware of my own discomforts, my Allius,*
> *and in case you might think that I am spurning the duty of a*
> *friend,*
> *hear what streams of misfortune I myself am sunk in and*
> *cease to seek the gifts of good fortune from one who is himself*
> *pitiful.*
> *When the white garment was first given to me,*   15
> *when my flowery time of life was exercising a pleasurable*
> *spring,*

then I played around quite enough. The goddess is not unaware
    of my existence,
that goddess who mingles sweet bitterness with passions.
But the death of my brother has removed all this enthusiasm
    with grief.
O brother, stolen from me in my misery,   20
dying you shattered my pleasures, brother,
our whole house is buried with you,
all our joys have perished along with you,
joys which your sweet love fed while you lived.
At his death I have banished right out of my mind   25
these enthusiasms and all pleasures of the mind.
So, when you write "Catullus, it is a disgrace for you to be in
    Verona",
because here anyone of higher quality
warms up his cold limbs in the bed you have deserted –
it is not a disgrace, my Allius, it is more a pitiful state of
    affairs.   30
Forgive me, therefore, if I do not send you these gifts
(of which grief has robbed me), since I am unable to send them.
The reason why I have no great abundance of writings with me
is that I live in Rome; that is my home,
that is my abode, there is my life spent –   35
only one out of many book-boxes follows me here.
That being so, I would hate you to deduce that I was doing this
    out of spite
or with a spirit which is less than generous
because you have up until now not received what you asked for:
if I had any sort of supply, I would give it you unasked. 40

Goddesses, I cannot keep silent about the matter in which
    Allius

assisted me, or the extent of the duties with which he fostered
   my cause,
in case time in its forgetful generations
should shroud this care of his in blind night:
but I will tell you, and you then tell many thousands   45
and make this old page of mine speak out

(gap in the manuscript)

and being dead may yet grow more and more famous,
and also so that the spider weaving its slender web up on high
may not make the deserted name of Allius into her next task. 50
For you know the passion which the perfidious Venus gave to
   me,
and the way in which she scorched me
when I was burning as much as the Trinacrian crag
and the Malian water in Thermopylae of Oeta,
when my sad eyes did not cease to melt with constant
   weeping   55
and my cheeks to be soaked with a shower of sadness,
just like a gleaming stream on the summit of a high hill
leaps out from a mossy stone –
a stream which when it has rolled straight down the sloping
   valley
passes over the middle of the road thronged with people,   60
a sweet refreshment for the wayfarer in his tired sweat
when heavy heat cracks open the burnt fields:
and also like when sailors are tossed about in a black storm,
a favourable breeze comes with gentler breath,
implored with prayers now to Pollux, now to Castor –   65
that was what Allius' help was like to me.
He opened up a closed field with a broad path,
he gave us a house, he gave a mistress,

where we might exercise our mutual love.
My gleaming goddess brought herself to it with delicate foot 70
and set her shining sole on the well-rubbed threshold,
standing there leaning on it with her sandal tapping on it,
just as once Laudamia, blazing with love for her husband,
came to the house of Protesilaus:
a house begun in vain, since the sacrificial victim had not yet 75
appeased the heavenly lords with its sacred blood.
May nothing please me so much, Nemesis the maiden of
    Rhamnus,
as to be undertaken rashly against the will of the gods.
How much the hungry altar yearns for the holy blood,
this was Laudamia taught when she lost her man, 80
forced to send away the embrace of her new husband before one
    winter and then again another winter
could have satisfied her greedy passion in its long nights,
to make her able to live with her marriage stolen from her –
a fact which the Fates knew was not far away 85
if he went as a soldier to the walls of Troy.
For at that time, with the stealing of Helen, Troy had begun
to draw to itself the leaders of the Greeks,
Troy (what wickedness!) the shared grave of Asia and of Europe,
Troy the bitter ashes of men and of all manly qualities, 90
Troy which also brought lamentable death to my brother.
Alas, brother stolen from me in my pitiful state,
alas the pleasant light of life stolen from my pitiful brother;
our whole house is buried with you,
all our joys have perished along with you, 95
joys which your sweet love fed while you lived.
Now so far away, not among the familiar tombs,
not laid to rest near the ashes of those known to you,
but held in filthy Troy, buried in unhappy Troy,

strange earth holds you on its furthest soil.   100
That was the place to which at that time <chosen> Greek youth
is said to have hurried from all sides, abandoning their homes
    and hearths,
to prevent Paris getting away with his stolen lover
and living a life of liberty and idleness in his war-free bedroom.
By that same misfortune, o most beautiful Laudamia,   105
your marriage was stolen from you, a marriage sweeter to you
    than your life
and your soul; the tide of love sucked you in so great a whirlpool
and dropped you into a precipitous pit,
just like the one the Greeks say is near Cyllenaean Pheneus
and dries out the rich soil with a drained marsh.   110
The false-parented son of Amphitryon, Hercules, is said
once to have dug this out by cutting out the heart of the
    mountain,
at that time when he shot down the Stymphalian monsters with
    his unerring
arrow on the orders of a master inferior to himself,
so that the doorway of heaven might be trodden by more
    gods   115
and to prevent Hebe from enduring a long virginity.
But your deep love was deeper than that pit,
a love which taught you – although not broken in yet – to bear
    the yoke.
Not so dear to a parent worn out with age,
is the head of a late grandson being fed by his one and only
    daughter: 120
the child has been found for his grandfather's wealth in the nick
    of time
and has had his name entered into the witnessed will,
putting a stop to the wicked joys of the foiled next of kin,

and shooing away the vulture from his white head.
Nor has any dove found such great happiness with his snowy
    mate –   125
although the dove is said to be much more shameless
than the most outstandingly promiscuous woman
in constantly plucking kisses with his nibbling beak.
But you alone outdid the great passions of all these,
when once you were joined with your fair-haired husband.   130
Totally or all but totally comparable to this woman,
my darling brought herself into my embrace,
with Cupid frequently darting around her, now here now there,
shining brilliantly in his saffron tunic.
She is not content with Catullus alone,   135
but we will put up with the infrequent infidelities of my modest
    mistress,
to prevent us being too much of a bore in the manner of stupid
    men.
Often even Juno, the greatest of the heaven-dwellers,
swallowed up her anger blazing at the misbehaviour of her
    husband,
realising that all-desiring Jupiter's lapses were
    multitudinous.   140
And yet it is not fair to compare human with divine,

(gap in the manuscript)

pick up the thankless burden of an aged parent.
She was not led down by the hand of her parent,
coming to the house which burned with Assyrian scent,
but rather she gave me stolen little gifts in the wonderful
    night-time,   145
gifts taken right from the very embrace of her very own
    husband.

And so it is enough, if to me alone is given
the day which she marks out with a brighter stone.
This is the gift, Allius, such as I could manage, finished off in
*   verse*
and given to you in return for many duties,   150
so that this day and then another, and then another and then
*   another*
may not touch your name with foul rust.
To this the gods will add as many as possible of the gifts which
*   Themis once*
was in the habit of bringing to good people of old.
May you be happy, both you and the love of your life,   155
and the house itself in which we sported, and my mistress too,
and Afer who first gave you to us,
the man from whose original goodness all I have now stems,
and far above all others she who is dearer to me than I am to
*   myself,*
my light, whose life makes living sweet.   160

A brief summary of this lengthy poem will help here:

	1–40	Allius asks for the poet's help, but the poet is himself wretched at his brother's death and so unable to supply the comfort his friend wants
a	41–50	Allius' gift of friendship
b	51–6	who gave the poet a house to meet his mistress
c	57–72	which gave him such ecstasy
d	73–86	Laudamia's love for Protesilaus
e	87–90	ended in his dying at Troy
f	91–100	as did Catullus' brother
e	101–4	Troy and separation

d 105–18 Laudamia's love thwarted

c 119–34 when before it was ecstatic

b 135–40 Catullus and his lover and the agony of infidelity

a 141–8 his lover's gift of love

   149–60 Conclusion

The summary printed above shows the arching ring-composition of the poem, whereby the poem unwinds itself and then rewinds the same themes in reverse order.

The poet mixes the topical and the universal, the contemporary and the mythical, love and grief, in a seamless synthesis. The theme of love (for his mistress, for his brother, of Laudamia for Protesilaus) mingles with that of grief tied by common elements such as Troy (where Protesilaus and the brother died) and the shared abode (Lesbia like Laudamia entering the home of the lover). There are also ironic contrasts between these elements which force the interpretation of the poem away from any simple 'moral' standpoint: Lesbia, for instance, is married, like Laudamia, but not to her lover: and the adultery of another married woman (Helen) caused the Trojan War and the death of Protesilaus (the moralising language of 103–4 is incongruous (not to say hypocritical) in the mouth of the poet whose own lover was also a married woman). Adultery is painful for the betrayed – even for the 'greatest of the heaven-dwellers' Juno (138) – but it can produce heroes such as Hercules whose own exploits are of great benefit to mankind (111–16). The death of the beloved is also painful (and Catullus is inconsolable about his own grief (19–24, 91–100)) but other people's grief is more readily explicable as frustrated passion (80–4). The gender correspondences of the *exempla* are teasingly inconsistent also: Catullus is a man in love with a woman, but he is time and again compared to the female in the role models adopted – he is Laudamia to his girlfriend's

Protesilaus, Laudamia to his brother's Protesilaus, Juno to his mistress's Jupiter.

The poem is more than a set of clever tricks of symmetry, however. There are the themes of the house – Laudamia is going to a real home when she marries Protesilaus while the poet takes his mistress to a borrowed home. Ironically (again) the home of Protesilaus will not provide a haven of happiness after the first winter and was in fact 'begun in vain' (75), while the poet's snatched happiness in a borrowed and uncertain abode makes his life worth living. On the other hand, the death of the poet's brother has destroyed his own home (22–3, 94–5). There are four views of sexual relationships here and they contrast neatly; that of Protesilaus and Laodamia (real marriage but unfulfilled), that of the poet and his mistress (not a real marriage and yet fulfilled), the union which produces the baby in 119–24 (real and fulfilled) and (28–9) the celibate life of the poet (unreal and unfulfilled). More important still is the theme of death.

Love and death were linked in poem 5, whose argument was that life is too short not to enjoy love. Poem 68 takes a much more profound look at this issue and sees the truth as being more complex. The poet can rescue the name of Allius from the decay and death of oblivion (45–50; cf. 151–2) but is still inconsolable at the death of his brother (91–6). The love of Laudamia and Protesilaus was doomed in the Trojan War which made Troy the 'shared tomb' of Asia and Europe – a war caused by the love of Helen and Paris. These coherences and ironies are obvious: the reader is led along a series of interconnected images and ideas without any single theme or 'moral', the simple message of gratitude towards Allius being both qualified and embodied in the poetic variation to which the poet subjects it.

More subtle still, however, is the poet's use of similes in the poem. Ever since Homer, poets had been composing similes in their narratives, for the effects of variation, of decoration, of analogy, even of proof (as in Lucretius). Singular experience – of death in battle, for instance – is compared to universal experience, often of the natural world of flowers, animals and the weather. Things we have not seen (such as the god Hermes) are compared to things we have seen which are superficially similar (such as the simile of the seagull in Homer, *Odyssey* 5.51–4). Lucretius uses the simile to allow the reader to visualise the invisible world of atoms in the visible world (of sheep on a hillside, for instance, at 2.317–22), or to demonstrate a scientific proposition (the optical illusions at 4.324–468 prove that the senses are nonetheless reliable) or combine science with a emotional edge (the pathetic image of the calf slaughtered in 2.350–66). Later Love Elegists often compare themselves and their beloved to figures from heroic legend: Propertius for instance sees himself as Milanion to Cynthia's Atalanta in his first poem. It is not enough for the poet to be himself; the love-poet uses the wider literary tradition to create elegy out of love. These comparisons elevate the ordinary world of the lover and his girlfriend into the extraordinary stuff of heroes, and sometimes also set up ironic contrasts – such as in Propertius 1.3. where the sleeping Cynthia is 'idealised' by her inebriated lover until she wakes and is terrifyingly 'real' and scolds him. Catullus in poem 68 sets up similes which do more than simply decorate a story with fairytales. In terms of sheer volume, there are more lines spent on similes in this poem than there are on the things which the similes are there to describe. In a very real sense, the similes are what the poem is all *about*.

For the choice of similes is bizarre: the poet selects his subjects with the obvious intention of surprising the reader, just as the labyrinthine thread of poem 64 startles the reader at every turn. Comparing the depth of Laudamia's love to a deep pit dug by Hercules or the glee of a grandfather is unusual and forces the reader to reassess at every turn the exact relationship between

the 'tenor' (i.e. the thing compared – e.g. Laudamia's love) and the
'vehicle' (the thing to which it is being compared, e.g. the pit). All
ancient poets are sensitive to the possibilities of subtle manipu-
lation of the reader by the delicate slippage between coherence and
contrast, between reinforcement of image and ironic questioning
of it. This becomes more urgent in this poem if only because of the
quantity of simile involved: in lines 41–160, 45 lines are 'straight'
simile. The simile comparing the poet's beloved with Laudamia
encloses its own similes to illuminate Laudamia's love, the simile
within the simile mirroring the poem within the poem. If we remove
the similes, there is precious little left here: Allius lent me a house
for love-making and my brother has died. Hardly enough to qualify
as 'gifts of the Muses and of Venus'.

The similes also shift focus constantly. The poet early on (53)
describes himself as blazing with passion like Mount Aetna or the
hot springs of Thermopylae – the fire of Aetna countered with the
water of the spring, but with a common element in both being heat:
this heat is then compared to that of a hot dry summer which a
spring relieves with its cool irrigation from the top of a mountain
(like Aetna?). So the figure of the heat becomes a figure of its cure,
the same elements (mountains and springs) being used to express
both heat and coolness. Add to this the reference to the poet's
tears and the simile takes on a further dimension of tears pouring
down his face (55–6) falling like a stream down a mountain. What
was first the hot water of passion or the volcanic mountain of fire
becomes the hot tears of a poet and then the cool mountain spring
refreshing the weary wayfarer. The wayfarer then gets more water
than he wants as he becomes a sailor out at sea desperate for the
storm wind to become a gentle breeze, the aid of the gods invoked
to deliver salvation, the similes brought to rest in the metaphor of
line 67 where Allius is said to have 'opened up a closed path' thus
concluding the wayfarer theme. This series of similes is especially

surprising if one recalls the tenor behind them: the poet's burning passion for his beloved, relieved by the loan of a house. The house is thus the cool stream to his Thermopylae of passion, the breeze to his storm, the gods invoked delivering his beautiful goddess (*candida diva* (70)). The sequence is elegant and seamless, but the extravagant vehicles are disproportionate to the tenor: whatever is going on here, the poet is not simply seeking to move the reader's sympathy for his plight.

The beloved arrives, and her foot is planted on the threshold. The poet then leaves her mid-step for sixty lines while he travels in time and space to Troy. The simile of Laudamia has obvious points of contact with the poet – love and the loss of a beloved at Troy – but many ironic elements. Laudamia is married to her lover, unlike the poet's mistress, who is unfaithful, while Laudamia is not: Laudamia's lost beloved is her husband, while Catullus' grief is for his brother: Laudamia's love was stolen from her as a result of Paris stealing the love of the adulterous Helen, which makes Catullus and his adulterous lover in fact closer to Paris and Helen than to the respectable Laudamia and Protesilaus. Within this lengthy simile are embedded other sub-similes such as that comparing the depth of Laudamia's love with the depth of the pit dug by Hercules – again, a simile rich in associative power when we recall that Hercules carried out the labour in order to win an immortal bride (just as Catullus had his goddess (*diva* (70)), and again a simile of ambiguous intent in the imagery of the pit: the Latin word *barathrum* more commonly denotes dismal death than joy, is more often a symbol of destruction rather than simply 'depth of feeling': the word is used frequently of 'the underworld' (as in Plautus, *Rudens* 570; Lucretius 3.966). In using a 'death' word to describe 'love' Catullus manages to unite the two themes of the central part of the poem – his love for his mistress and his grief for his brother – and then caps it by denying that the simile is adequate to describe the love anyway (117). The

poet then adds two more similes – the late-born grandson and the
wanton dove – neither of which is an ideal vehicle but both of which
add a great deal to the texture of the poem. The late-born grandson
presents an idyllic picture of family life which succeeds in foiling
the villainous legacy-hunter and maintains the family inheritance
with unbroken fidelity: this hardly has any direct bearing either
on Laudamia (who has no children) or on the poet's lover (who
is contaminating her family inheritance by her affair with the
poet). Again, the point of comparison – the joy and delight – is
almost swallowed in the mass of extraneous and oblique detail.
The dove is even more oblique – her promiscuity recalling that of
Catullus' youth (17) and also of his mistress (135–6), her ambiguity
shown in the clash between her love for her mate and her wanton
reputation. To make the irony even more acute, the dove is called
compar – meaning both 'mate' and also 'similar' – the poet thus
referring to the process of comparison in the middle of his simile,
a gesture of self-conscious allusion. Once again, the poet ends by
rejecting the simile as a suitable description of Laudamia – 'you
outdid the great passions of all these ...' (129) just as he has done
over the pit (117) and just as he will do in referring his mistress to
Laudamia (131). The poet constantly shifts the focus of our vision
and constantly draws our attention both to the process itself and to
its inadequacy. Nor, finally, is this merely arch pretentiousness.
The figure of the poet's married lover is seen from different oblique
perspectives in a manner which lies at the heart of what the poem
is trying to do. When she first appears she is not human at all – she
is his 'gleaming goddess' (70) as she sets her foot on the threshold.
When she crosses the threshold sixty lines later she is still seen
in mythical terms with Cupid flitting about her (133–4), but the
romance is at once dashed by the poet's honesty about her lack
of fidelity – she is not even faithful in her adultery, let alone her
marriage. Her former status of 'goddess' is revised in the light of

this and she becomes Jupiter to his Juno – appallingly promiscuous and a source of anger to her beloved – rather than Hebe to his Hercules. The simile of Laudamia which appeared to be showing the idyll of the poet's love in fact showed the opposite. The only things which he had in common with Laudamia were his grief – grief born of love, and all the more painful for that – and his sexual desire. The legend of love and heroism in the similes is shattered in the grim realisation of the truth: his 'wife' is somebody else's wife, his house is somebody else's house, his own home is one of loneliness, grief and frustration (27–35). The bliss of the poem is based on a lie.

And yet the poem does not end on a note of disillusion. Far from it: she is his 'light' who makes his life worth living. For all her manifest faults she is as flesh and blood preferable to the tissue of plaster heroines and nature-similes with which he has been comparing her throughout the poem. The closure of the poem brings us back to the real world, just as do the codas of poems 63, 64 and 66. The end result is a delicious irony whereby the reader – having been entertained and moved by a sequence of dazzling poetic inspiration – is finally convinced that the slippage in this poem is not simply between the tenor and the vehicle of the many similes but goes deeper than that: it is between the language of poetry and the language of truth, between the image of the beloved held in anticipation of her visit and the reality of the love-making itself – an act which Catullus (himself no prude) did not describe – between the world of fantasy and the world of myth. The poet's grief for his brother is of course part of the 'real world' – and is not subjected to the sort of comparisons which Lesbia receives – and acts as a counterweight to the legend of heroic death; Troy contrasted with the brute truth about real death in Troy. This is not a didactic 'message' against poetry – that would be absurd. What the poet leaves us with is the sense that poetry has the power to transform the everyday and the banal into the purest fantasy; and that the value of the poetry lies not in its fidelity to historical truth but rather in its own hermetic world of language and of sensitivity. At the end of this poem we are left with a poet having it both ways: to close a gloriously successful piece of poetic imagination he leaves us with a self-deprecating glimpse of the reality which transcends the poem which has embodied it.

CHAPTER 4

DOCTUS POETA –
THE USES OF LEARNING

Only as an aesthetic phenomenon can the world be justified –
Nietzsche *Die Geburt der Tragödie*

Catullus, like many Roman poets, was 'learned' (*doctus*) and many of his poems read like highly crafted and skilled exercises in poetic technique and mythological allusion. This may come as something of a surprise to some readers. Catullus is, after all, popular in many Latin courses because he is *not* soaked in learned allusions. Many of his shorter poems in particular are direct, personal and instantly accessible to anyone. This is true – but to concentrate solely on these poems would be to close our eyes to much of the greatest poetry in the collection. This chapter will look in some detail at poems 63 and 64 in an attempt to see both the intelligence of the poetry and also the pleasure to be gained from reading and understanding these texts.

Catullus' longest poem is his mini-epic poem (64) on the marriage of Peleus and Thetis. The poem begins by taking one mythological tale – the meeting and then the wedding of the human Peleus and the divine sea-goddess Thetis, and their future offspring Achilles – but he inserts into this tale another story, namely that of Ariadne abandoned on the island of Naxos by her faithless lover Theseus and rescued by the god Bacchus. The poem plays tricks on the reader all the time; the opening lines

> Once upon a time, pine trees grown on the peak of mount
>   Pelion
> swam they say through the liquid waves of Neptune
> to the streams of Phasis and the territory of Aeetes ...

make us immediately assume that the poem is going to tell the
story of Jason and the Golden Fleece, but this expectation is soon
foiled as we focus on one sailor of the Argo to the exclusion of
the others and not on the voyage on which they were engaged.
The sea nymphs had never before seen such a thing as a ship
on their seas and so were off their guard when it came into
view; the sailors for the first and last time in human history saw
these nymphs 'bare of body, standing out of the white torrent
up to their breasts' (17–18) and Peleus and Thetis were mutually
smitten. The wedding is arranged and gods and humans all turn
up to felicitate the happy pair with gifts. Central to the marriage
bedroom is (of course) the bed – and the coverlet which is on
this bed tells a much more sinister tale. The picture on it shows a
triptych which the large central digression of the poem maps out
in great detail; at one extreme there is Theseus sailing away from
Naxos looking towards his homeland of Athens, in the centre is
Ariadne gazing longingly and desperately at her departing lover,
while behind her is the figure of the god Bacchus who has seen
her and is coming to rescue her. This digression to describe a work
of art or a landscape was known in ancient times as an *ecphrasis*
and the first example of the genre was Homer's long description
of the shield of Achilles in *Iliad* book 18. Usually this sort of
digression is a fraction of a much longer epic – in Homer's case
less than 1% of the whole poem. In Catullus 64 the 'digression'
takes up 214 lines of a poem which is only 408 lines long in all
– more than half the text is thus 'digression' and terms such as
'digression' begin to lose their point. We saw a similar inversion

of proportions in poem 68 where the similes take up more space than the story. Nor is this the only surprise in the poem.

It is not particularly appropriate to talk about divorce at a wedding, and for the marriage bed of Peleus and Thetis to show a woman abandoned by her lover might be seen as similarly tactless. When we 'see' the whole picture, we will see that Ariadne is in fact rescued by a god; so the wedding guests thus have a privileged access to the 'moral' point being made (namely that marrying a god, as Peleus is doing, is a better bet than marrying a human). The hapless woman herself (and the reader) is unaware of Bacchus until the end of the passage; and she expresses her feelings of anger and despair in an impassioned speech directed at the fleeing figure of Theseus. Again, this is not what one expects. Quite apart from the fact that pictures do not speak and so the poet is animating the inanimate or (in modern terms) turning the still life into a film, there is the faint threat in Ariadne's words that love may well be marvellous but that when it goes wrong it produces despair and suffering and (in her own case) the danger of death itself. Once again, things are not what they seem. She strips her clothing off in a well-described striptease:

> not keeping the delicate headband on her blonde head,
> not keeping her breast veiled and concealed with the light
>   robe,
> not binding her milky breasts with the flimsy bra –
> all of which slipped right off her whole body in all
>   directions. (63–6)

This certainly keeps the (male) reader entertained but its purpose is hardly titillation of Theseus as some scholars assume; it is rather a gesture of grief and abandonment such as the desperation of Andromache whose grief at the death of her husband Hector makes her partially disrobe:

> Far from her head she threw the gleaming headband
> the diadem, the cap, the holding-band all woven
> and the circlet which golden Aphrodite had once given her.
>   Homer, *Iliad* 22.468–70

There is of course irony at work here also; she is showing her beauty to the god behind her whom she cannot see but who can see her and who will rescue her, turning her present grief into future joy.

She curses men in general ('from now on let no woman believe a man's oath or expect a man's words to be reliable; so long as their lustful heart is ardent to get something there is nothing that men will not swear ... but once their lust has been slaked then they have no fear of breaking their oaths ...' 143–8) and Theseus in particular, and curses in ancient poetry usually come true. Theseus duly goes home to Athens but forgets to change the sails on his ship – the agreed sign to tell his father that he was coming home safe and sound – and so poor old Aegeus throws himself off a cliff in grief for his supposedly dead son. So the Greek hero's intended victim (Ariadne) is in fact saved while his unintended victim (Aegeus) is doomed. The poet even remonstrates with Love the god and Venus his mother:

> Alas, divine boy, who stir up madness sadly with your
>   ruthless heart
> who mixes together human joys and human sorrows,
> and you lady who rule over Golgi and leafy Idalium –
> on what streams did you toss the girl, on fire in her mind
> sighing again and again over the fair-haired foreigner!
>   (94–8)

This is (again) not the most tactful image to present to a couple on their wedding day, and scholars have argued for many years about whether the poem is 'really' optimistic or pessimistic, whether it is an attack on marriage masquerading as an idyll or whether it is merely a clever poem. In the context of the wedding of Peleus and Thetis of course there is no problem. Ariadne *has* been abandoned by Theseus and she *thinks* that her life is over, but we know that the god Bacchus is about to take her off on his tiger-driven chariot for a life of immortal bliss; a god will be much better than a human, seems to be the message of the story, and Peleus is marrying a god. So there is nothing technically inappropriate about the coverlet. But what of the long lament which shows Ariadne's despair at the infidelity of men?

Again, this can be seen as dramatic irony, in the sense that her sorrow is expressed for all it is worth so that her subsequent bliss will be all the greater. This is the sort of teasing irony which we find (for instance) in the last book of Homer's *Odyssey* where the returning hero lets his old and sick father assume that his son is still lost, only to reveal himself as very much present and alive. The consequent happiness is all the greater for the depths of despair which preceded it. This does not work so well in the present case, however, as we do not see and can only infer the actual meeting of Ariadne and Bacchus and their subsequent happiness has to be assumed. If the point of the passage were that 'all shall be well' then the poet has omitted the vital conclusion. Theseus and Ariadne's expectations are all foiled. He thinks he is coming home to a rapturous welcome when in fact he comes home to his father's funeral:

> so, entering the dwelling of his home which was mourning
>   for his father's
> death, fierce Theseus received the sort of grief which
> in his forgetfulness of mind he had inflicted on the
>   daughter of Minos. (246–8)

while her expectation of imminent death will also be foiled in this most blissful denouement – but the poet chooses not to dwell on

that, leaving us instead with what he can see on the coverlet of
Bacchus and his train:

> Yet from elsewhere, flowery Bacchus was flying
> with his group of Satyrs and Sileni born on Mount Nysa,
> looking for you, Ariadne, and on fire with passion for you
>   ... (251–3)

This is not the end of the poem, either. As we return to the wedding
of Peleus and Thetis there enter the Fates, who are grotesquely ugly
and whose role is to sing the future. They duly predict the future
child of this union: the greatest of the Greek heroes, Achilles, a man
who will be a terrifying killing machine when he gets to Troy, whose
acts of homicide will leave many a mother weeping and the rivers
choked with blood:

> that man's outstanding heroism and famous deeds
> will often be spoken of by mothers at their sons' funeral
> when they will loose their unkempt hair from their hoary
>   head
> and will bruise their decaying breasts with feeble hands ...
> the wave of Scamander will testify to his immense
>   heroism ...
> whose stream he will choke with heaps of bodies,
>   slaughtered.
> warming the deep river with mingled blood ... (348–51,
>   357, 359–60)

The climax of Theseus' heroism was to abandon a helpless girl to
death on Naxos, the culmination of Achilles' 'heroism' will be that
over his tomb the Trojan girl Polyxena will be slain as a human
sacrifice. So the Cretan princess Ariadne was abandoned to death
by one Greek hero, and here we see another foreign princess being
slaughtered to honour a dead Greek. The marriage will produce pain

and suffering on an epic scale – so again the poet is showing the many different sides of the same scene. So the wedding of Peleus and Thetis looks wonderful but is going to produce misery, while the abandoning of Ariadne by Theseus looks miserable but is going to produce bliss when Bacchus comes along, as he is the god whose rites are ecstatic as the poet reminds us:

> (Bacchus' followers) were raging wildly with distracted
>   minds,
> shouting 'evoe' in tumult, 'evoe' as they bent back their
>   heads ... (254–5)

Nothing, it seems, can be taken at face value – behind the façade of the picture or the poem there is no certainty, but the last page of the poem is perhaps the greatest surprise of them all.

The poem ends with a highly moralistic epilogue in which the poet purports to lament the decline of morals in his own day.

> For in earlier times the heaven-dwellers used to visit
> the pure homes of heroes in person and show themselves
> to human gathering since religion had not yet been
>   spurned.
> Often the father of the gods visited his gleaming temple
> when the annual rites had come round on festival days
> and saw a hundred bulls crash to the ground.
>   ...
> But after the earth was soaked with evil crime
> and everybody dispelled justice from their lustful minds,
> brothers wet their hands with brothers' blood,
> the son stopped grieving for his deceased parents,
> the father longed for the death of his first-born son
> so that he might be able freely to enjoy the flower of a new
>   young wife:

the wicked mother laying herself underneath her unwitting
son,
wickedly showing no fear of adulterating her family gods.
Everything speakable and unspeakable, mixed together in
wicked madness,
has turned the righteous minds of the gods away from us.
That is why they do not deem our such gatherings worthy
of a visit,
nor do they allow themselves to be touched with the clear
light of day. (384–408)

Nowadays, the poet tells us, we commit so many terrible sins
that the gods will not allow themselves to be seen by us, whereas
in the heroic age the gods went to Peleus' wedding and rescued
Ariadne from Naxos. The old association of gods and humans
has been broken by our wickedness. This epilogue has structural
value in that we end where we began with the miracle of gods
and humans sharing the same space and seeing each other; it also
has thematic value in that it explains why this tale could never
happen today. Nobody takes this epilogue at face value, seeing it
as evidence that the real Catullus believed that the real gods would
talk to him in person if only the real Romans were not so wicked.
On the other hand, scholars have been ready to see it as proof
that this poem is being used by the poet as a stick to beat his own
age, without seeing that this moralistic reading would only work if
the poet used language which his readers could accept instead of
arguing that the gods really would come down to see us. Secondly,
his choice of moral vices to blame is decidedly odd: rather than
listing the very real public crimes which real Romans went in for
on a large scale – judicial murder, perjury and so on – he gives
us a saga of more exotic family evils. He tells us that it is crimes
such as incest between mother and son, brothers murdering each

other, fathers wanting the death of their children to leave them more able to marry again. These are sins which one can find in the pages of Cicero – pro Cluentio has quite a few of them in the outrageous career of Oppianicus, for instance – but it is hard to see the poet as inveighing against real life in this moralistic way when the premise of the argument ('once upon a time gods and men met up') is so hard to sustain. The sins listed are against blood relations and recall the world of Greek Tragedy and blood guilt, and the lament over the loss of justice is all too similar to earlier Greek literature to be taken at face value. The wistful longing for the old days of free association of men and gods recalls Homer (Odyssey 7.201–6) where king Alcinous claims that:

> in the past the gods have always appeared plain to see as gods when we sacrifice sumptuous hecatombs, and they feast sitting with us where we sit. Even when a lonely traveller meets them they make no concealment, for we are close to them.

and the link between divine presence and human morals is also made by Hesiod, who in the Works and Days has a catalogue of the degeneration of the human race from its age of gold to the present day with its lack of moral justice; a later poet Aratus used the departure of Justice from the earth to explain the origin of he constellation Virgo – Justice could not bear our appalling behaviour any more and fled to the heavens. The motif lived on – a drunken guest at Trimalchio's table (Petronius, Satyrica 44) laments that in the old days women prayed for rain and it came down in buckets, while now the fields lie parched Again, the use of literacy is that one can here see the poet reading and re-interpreting the poetry of the past and recreating it in his own poetry. It allows him to bring his legendary tale of the heroic age right up to date – to 'us' (line 406) – bringing the past to the present, but it does so in a form of words which has been used before and which therefore casts itself into inverted commas rather than being the poet's own views. This is not to say that Catullus had no moral views – just that he used moralising language here to end this cryptic poem on a suitably cryptic note. The style of the nostalgic passage is overblown epic – the gods are called 'heaven-dwellers', the rich poetic proper names lend an air of legend to the whole thing – while the incensed moralism of the final twelve lines is also rich in overdone epithets. The 'earth' is 'soaked' with 'evil crime', parents want children to die and children want parents to die, 'normal' marriages being pushed aside for the unnaturally young bride and the incest of mother and son. The poet is still master of his technique – but its use in this context is more richly ironic than heartfelt. There is also abundant and pleasing symmetry in the whole passage – the 'father of the gods' (i.e. Jupiter) is contrasted with the wicked father of a son he wants dead, the god Bacchus is called by his cult title Liber ('free') to contrast with the father who wants to be 'free' to marry his young bride without the inconvenient son around. The last couplet uses the telling word *coetus* for 'gatherings'; this word then as now also had the sense of 'sexual congress' and reminds us that the two mythological sexual unions of human and divine which the poem has described are being alluded to. We might also remember the many other 'unions' of human and divine which caused such misery and mayhem in the legendary past – the poet's blithe optimism about the justice of the gods and the desirability of such 'unions' would not impress (say) Semele whose union with Jupiter produced a son Bacchus for him and death for her, or Io whose seduction ended up with her being turned into a cow to escape the jealous eyes of Jupiter's wife Juno, or Alcmene who was tricked by a randy Jupiter into betraying her husband (thus being Lucretia to his Tarquin). Gods in myth do these shocking things simply because they can. The poet's tissue of theological optimism falls at the first close inspection. So why end the poem like this? Perhaps – and like all readings, this one is inevitably only a 'perhaps' – the final passage is a reminder that we are here *not* dealing in didactic moralism in this poem. What is on first glance a moral 'comment' turns out to be a stance, a pose like any other. This may be a 'signature' to mark the end of the poem but the person speaking is still the narrator and (like all narrators) is not always to be trusted. The poem has shown us the love of human and divine from a variety of angles and illuminated the old stories of Peleus and of Ariadne with his own 'bright light of day'. Poetry, the epilogue now tells us, is the only 'light' which can illuminate these tales as they cannot happen in real life any more. The moralistic reasons he gives may be spurious but the conclusion is ultimately literary rather than theological or moral. Art can shine a clear light where real life is dark and dirty; only aesthetically can we appreciate the world of myth and legend, as the gods are hidden there. Only the poet can let us see them with the 'clear light of day'. Perhaps, as Nietzsche was later to claim in *The Birth of Tragedy*, it is only as an aesthetic phenomenon that the world can be justified.

Poem 63 is quite unique. For one thing it is composed in one of the hardest of Latin metres, the galliambics; this rhythm – the one used by the Galli of priests of the Great Goddess Cybele in their hymns to her – demands that 10 of the 16 syllables in each line be short – and if that were not hard enough, four of the short syllables have to run consecutively. So the first line has *rate maria* which is five short syllables. This kind of metrical demand is hard to do at all. To keep it going for 93 lines is a real *tour de force*.

Secondly, the narrative of the poem is bizarre to say the least. It tells the tale of one Attis who, in his desire to become one with the Great Goddess whom he worships, castrates himself. The poem serves as something of an aetiological myth to explain the institution of the eunuch priesthood which worshipped Cybele, but the suggestion that it was written specifically for the *Ludi Megalenses* (celebrated in April in honour of Cybele) goes beyond any available evidence. The figure of Attis is (besides) hardly one of heroism; he ends the poem lamenting his sorry new state and fleeing back to the woods when driven there by a lion which has been set upon him by the goddess he venerates.

The poem may well be a good example of what happens when a poet tries out a new metrical or poetic form. We often imagine that poets sit down in a blaze of emotional inspiration and pour out their feelings into the most appropriate form: but it may be that (as Wilde asserted in *The Critic as Artist*) that 'the real artist is he who proceeds, not from feeling to form, but from form to thought and passion'; in other words, the poet sits down and begins to compose in a metre such as galliambics, and finds that in the course of composition he discovers feelings in himself which the poem brings to expression. The poet did not sit down in order to express them but the text becomes the vehicle of the words which his artistry finds and the feelings come with the words.

The text under discussion here is certainly complex and rewarding. It is a poem of polar contrasts: the western Greek and the eastern Phrygian, the sophisticated city and the wild woods, the humble devotion of the mortal male and the proud arrogance of the divine female, the spoiled and popular youth with bands of followers becoming a wretched and lonely exile (notice how the companions disappear without comment, their purpose being solely to contrast popularity and loneliness), the beloved young man becoming a heartbroken lover of the unlovable Cybele, and so on; above all in its narrative drive this is a poem where rabid madness turns in the cold light of day to sick regret – a pattern familiar from such tragedies as Euripides' *Heracles* and Sophocles' *Ajax*, in both of which a goddess drives a mortal mad and he commits irreversible acts of violence which ruin his life.

The poet gives us three narrative standpoints: Attis as seen by his companions, Attis as he then sees himself, finally Attis as seen by the goddess and the lion. The heroic self-mutilator becomes a tragic figure of sad regret, only to become a farcical figure running away from an animal who has been told not to harm him; the poet plays with the responses of the reader, forcing us to abandon our critical conclusions as soon as we have formed them and leaving our emotions moved but confused.

Ironic clues are planted in many places: Attis' speech to his companions is dramatically ironic in the light of later events: he unconsciously reveals the excess (17) and folly (18) of these 'exiles' (14 – he is doomed to become a permanent exile himself) who are the 'wandering flocks' (*vaga pecora* (13) – animal imagery looking forward to the lion later) seeking what is not rightly theirs (14). His sentimental picture of the joys of worship in the woods (20-5) is shattered by the reality both of his situation (53-4, 68-72) and of his dread mistress (78-84), just as the dreamy picture of Phrygian revels is broken with the final word, the specifically Roman 'leaping dances' (*tripudiis*). They should hasten in dancing, Attis claims; but the only member of the goddess' coterie whom he actually encounters is the savage lion who makes only too sure that he 'hastens' (*celerare*) where the goddess wants him.

His second speech employs similar rhetoric to different ends, the extended repetition of 'where ... where ...' in 21-5 becoming the repetition of 'I ... I ... I ... I ...' in 68-71 as the unthinking hero becomes aware of his awful state, terms which he had idealised becoming terms of bitter regret (e.g. *Maenades* 23 – *Maenas* 69, *Phrygiam* 20 – *Phrygiae* 71), the heroic becoming the tragic. Even here, however, our emotions are kept in check by the poet's ingenuity – the constant use of feminine endings to describe the emasculated male, the breathless string of self-descriptions (63), the rising pattern of:

I Maenad, I a part of myself, I to be a sexless man? (69)

and especially the irony of 'part of myself' (*mei pars* – he has lost a part of himself – this is inverted into the conceit that what is left of him is only a part of himself); the high-flown language of compound adjectives (this aesthete cannot simply complain about the animals without describing them as 'wood-wandering stag ... grove-wandering boar' (*cerva silvicultrix ... aper nemorivagus* 72), the florid sensuous language describing his former florid sensuous lifestyle (64–7) and the mock-tragic wailing of

> pathetic, ah pathetic – again and again you must lament
> like this, o my heart

> *miser a miser, querendum est etiam atque etiam, anime* (61)

with that final 'o, my heart' a delicious ironical stance. It is also difficult to read lines 58–67 with much sympathy: the effete self-indulgent tone of the speech is self-parody of the foppish and spoiled youth who only has himself to blame for his plight and whose complaints after his self-inflicted injury are couched in plangent self-pity calculated to distance the emotions of the reader. Furthermore, there are plenty of negative aspects to his character: he has rejected Venus (17), he is like a heifer which has not been broken in and so is useless for farm work (33), or even worse a runaway slave leaving his master (51) – none of them calculated to win sympathy from a Roman audience.

Attis is not, then, an overwhelmingly attractive figure – but the divine heroine is no better. Cybele's speech is a parody of the 'angry god' figure; she uses the lash of madness (*furor* – a term often used of the madness of love) to halt Attis' flight for freedom (80) – but the madness which will drive him back is not the mad enthusiasm with which he mutilated himself, but simply blind panic in the face of a roaring lion. We thus imagine Attis from then on as being imprisoned in the woods by fear – bitter and resentful in the knowledge that he has thrown his life away. It would have been far kinder of the goddess to drive Attis mad and restore him to the frame of mind of lines 1–38, in which he was quite happy to serve her all his life; but then, kindness is not Cybele's strong point – she is herself a victim of the madness of anger as she shouts out with rhetorical repetition and alliteration:

> *agedum, inquit, age ferox, i fac ut hanc furor agitet*
> *fac uti furoris ictu ...*

> 'Go' she said 'make your way, fierce one, make madness stir
>   her on,
>   with the lash of madness make her return ...' (78–9)

and even the poor lion is made to suffer self-flagellation with his tail to serve the vindictive lusts of his mistress. Everybody suffers for her sake, and her vengeance is – as so often with avenging gods in classical mythology – unnecessary. Attis has mutilated himself irreversibly and will hardly be able to settle back into the urban life which he recollects wistfully. His 'excess of freedom' has been to regret his actions, and for this he will be locked up in fear and poverty for the rest of his life. The goddess shows herself to be a 'great mistress' (91) indeed, to be feared rather than admired. The ending of the story thus overturns the beginning, where Cybele was seen through the rosy spectacles of the infatuated Attis, and substitutes for the fairy godmother a hideous witch. Her portrayal is also ironically Roman and the language is very Roman – even the lion charges like a Roman soldier (*facit impetum* 89). The effect is not, however, political or even moral, but again ironic and distancing.

The poet's prayer at the end is a reaction to the story rather than a hymnic act of piety but then, the final three lines are the supreme

irony in the poem. A common form of closure in ancient poetry is
to end with a personal touch bringing the poem back to the present
and the truth (see e.g. Horace, *Epode* 2) as a distancing device almost
equivalent to the poet 'signing off'. So here, the notion of Catullus
emasculating himself and being chased into the woods by a lion
is patently ridiculous and sets the story we have heard into the
perspective of reality, especially as the poet (speaking apparently *in
propria persona*) uses the sort of language which Attis himself used
in order to mimic and therefore mock the tone of the story.

In structure, the poem falls into two distinct halves: Attis' act of
self-castration on day one (1–38), and his futile attempt to escape
and his expression of repentance on day two (39–90), rounded off
with a personal comment by the poet. The poem contains three
speeches: Attis to his companions (12–26), Attis to himself (50–73)
and finally Cybele to her lion (78–83). Each day begins with an
11-line narrative followed by a speech from Attis; on day one the
reaction is to run towards the goddess, on day two the reaction is to
flee from her. The symmetry and the balance of the poem are thus
abundantly clear, and the final effect is the representation of a state
of unbalanced mind in a poem of sublimely balanced artistry.

CHAPTER 5

OBSCENITY AND
HUMOUR

The previous chapter looked at two of the sublime and poignant longer poems of Catullus. Many readers, however, remember Catullus from their years of learning Latin because he is often neither sublime nor solemn. This chapter will look at the exuberant uses of humour and obscenity in the poetry.

Editing and publishing Catullus was always difficult in the past owing to the obscenity of some of his poems. Older editions (and not so old, such as that of Fordyce in 1961) simply omitted the offending poems altogether. The older Loeb edition would leave the rudest Latin untranslated or replace Catullus' original with discreet rows of dots. We may now wonder what all the fuss was about, until we read the poems themselves. Here is a particularly good example of the kind of poem which the older editors found it impossible to print.

> God help me – I never thought it made any difference
> whether it was Aemilius' mouth or his arsehole which I
>   smelt.
> The one is no cleaner, the other no dirtier;
> in fact the arsehole is cleaner and better –
> at least it has got no teeth. His mouth has teeth a foot and
>   a half long
> and gums like the ones an old wagon-box might have,

and a grin besides like the split open cunt
of a mule pissing in the summer.
He fucks loads of girls and thinks he is god's gift
and yet is not handed over to the mill and the donkey?
Surely we should think that any woman who touches him
could lick the arsehole of a hangman with diarrhoea?
   Poem 97

This poem – like all of ancient poetry – is skilfully composed in
a strict metrical pattern and sounds a great deal more ordered in
Latin than my fairly literal version above. There are some points of
detail which need investigating – the reference to the mill and the
donkey in line 10 presumably refers to the labouring of a donkey
pulling a pole which rotates a millstone and Aemilius' role would be
the boring one of overseeing the donkey at its work. The man who is
seen as a man-about-town in line 9 is really only fit for slavery – and
perhaps donkeys would not mind his appalling personal hygiene.
The wagon-box image is slightly odd but the reading of the Latin
goes back to Quintilian and so if the reading is wrong then it was a
very early corruption of the text.

The poem begins in studied disinterest – it does not matter which
end of Aemilius you smell, as both are horrible. This is pretty bad
to start with; then it turns out that it does matter as (contrary to
what one would expect) the anus is cleaner than the mouth. The
caricature continues with the comically less shocking revelation that
his anus has no teeth – which leads the poet into a lively and highly
imaginative description of the man's mouth. The caricature reaches
its peak in the ghastly picture of a mule (hardly the most appealing
of animals) pissing in summer (when one assumes that dehydration
would make the urine especially smelly and foul) and thus showing
its cunt 'split open'. This repellent image is contained in lines of
perfectly grammatical and regular Latin:

praeterea rictum qualem diffissus in aestu
meientis mulae cunnus habere solet.

The contrast between the appalling content and the elegance of the form is striking – and Catullus clearly intends both to shock and to impress his readers. The final couplet adds the suitably extreme touches which this poem needs to round it off: the final line consists of four words, each of them adding to the shock of the scene; it is a dysinteric man (*aegroti*) whose arse she could lick – and what is more he is a hangman / executioner (the sort of man that nice girls would not consort with at all, let alone do this sort of thing).

Is this a poem at all? Is it any good? Some readers might well see little to make this poem any better than the graffiti scrawled on lavatory walls. Few would give this poet a Nobel prize for this sort of verse. Why should we read it at all?

The answers are many. In the first place, we read it in the same way that we would read all the jottings and fragments of any writer whose work interests us. Secondly, we need to examine our own assumptions: Catullus himself (or his 'publisher') saw fit to put this poem into the Little Book which contains all that remains of this poet's work. The poem before this one (96) is a lovely poem of consolation for his friend Calvus on the loss of his Quintilia. Poem 101 is a famous and much quoted elegy on the death of the poet's own brother. Catullus clearly saw no loss of quality in these different poems and must have regarded poem 97 as being just as worthy of inclusion as poem 96. If we disagree (as well we may) then we need to look deeper at the reasons behind the ancient tradition of scatological invective to see why Catullus did not agree with us. Thirdly, this poem achieves something which a lot of poetry signally fails to achieve; it turns what is gross into something elegant and ordered, and it manages to surprise the reader by the clash of form and content and by the sheer verve of the poet's outrageous imagination. It is less difficult to write predictable poems about pretty girls and sunsets, and such verse will be hard pressed to surprise the reader; composing a piece of verse such as this which manages to insult somebody in the strongest possible language and yet remain within the limits of the Latin elegiac couplet is surprising. So is this poem merely scurrilous verse? Does it have any claim to be fine poetry? This last is ultimately going to be a matter of taste for the critic, but the same stylistic devices which so impress us in 'serious' poems like 76 are also to be found in this unlikely context. There is the neat closure whereby the 'mouth versus anus' point both opens and closes the poem, which could be described as an example of ring composition; there is the use of rhetorical repetitions ('cleaner ... cleaner ...; teeth ... teeth', etc); the long teeth being described with a suitably long word (*sesquipedalis* here translated 'a foot and a half long') and the monstrously ingenious obscenities described above. Few collections of poetry are without their lighter items and Catullus knew – as did Horace in the next generation – how to mingle the sublime and the ridiculous. Life is (after all) not all serious and not all solemn – and the talented poet can make poetry out of anything at all. Only the weak poet relies on tired old formulas and derivative poetic forms.

It is my contention that this sort of light verse is primarily humorous and this chapter will show how Catullus uses sexual and scatological humour to entertain his readers.

Of course the sort of scatology which we find here is not particularly novel, and (I suspect) would not have been particularly shocking to the Roman audience brought up on racier stuff than some of his editors were. In what follows I will try to trace the roots of Catullus' comic invective in earlier poetry of the ancient world.

In the first place there is the whole tradition of satire which goes back to Aristophanes in Athens in the fifth century BCE. His fantastic plays often involve scathing and obscene abuse of known individuals – to take one example out of many the leading politician Cleon is reduced in the *Knights* to a sycophantic bully. At one point (364) his rival the sausage seller threatens him: 'I will fuck your arsehole like a sausage-case' and later (1010) tells him to 'go and bite off his own cock'. Politicians, one may feel, are fair game as they put themselves up for office; less deserving is someone like the hapless Cleisthenes whose only crime was his inability to grow a beard. For this he was pilloried as a pathic homosexual, a coward, an effeminate and generally amusing in ways that we would regard as unfair and (now) politically incorrect. Abuse is part of the fun of comedy – what Dover (*Aristophanic Comedy* (London 1972) 31–41) called 'self-assertion' of the audience against all those people (and gods) who stand in authority over us. This sort of public humiliation finds a ready ear in all of us and needs a brave sort of society to allow it to happen at all. Less public is the world of satire.

'Satire is all ours' said Quintilian, by which he meant it was something which the Romans invented. Satire also takes on named individuals and types of individual and subjects them to ridicule for their folly and their vices. Catullus is in the tradition of the great Roman satirist Lucilius in some ways, but there is a fundamental difference between a poem like Catullus 97 and satire. Satire is – in Horace's famous phrase (*Satires* 1.1.24) – a matter of 'telling the truth with a smile' and generally involves making moralistic points through the medium of humour. It is the making of comments on the behaviour of others and uses laughter to effect its purposes. Now obviously some of the time the satirist is striking a pose, affecting strong moral feelings which he may not in fact have; one often feels with Juvenal for instance that the poems are the scripts of a performance in which the speaker is being held up to ridicule rather than his subject matter. The pretence of moralism is there, however. Catullus is not doing this. There is no moral flavour in poem 97 that I can detect. It is more in the tradition of the bitter

invective which we find in Horace's early *Epodes*. Look for instance
at number 8 of that collection:

> You dare to ask me, you decrepit smelly slag why I am
>   impotent?
> You with your black teeth, wrinkles ploughing your aged
>   forehead,
> your crude dirty arsehole gaping between your wizened
>   buttocks like a cow.
> Your floppy breasts stimulate me – I have seen bigger tits
>   on a horse
> your wobbly belly and skinny thighs on top of your swelling
>   ankles ...

This style of poetry goes back to that of the Greeks who also wrote
elegies of shocking obscenity and variety in the seventh and sixth
centuries BCE. One of these poets, Hipponax, invented the metrical
form of the scazon which Catullus was to use, while another great
Greek poet of the day, Archilochus, speaks frankly of his own (real or
imagined) disreputable behaviour. The story goes that Archilochus'
scathing poetic abuse of Lycambes and his daughters caused them
all to hang themselves in shame. The recently discovered Cologne
fragment of Archilochus shows the poet seducing the younger sister
of his girlfriend; the poem has sexual frankness as he describes his
success and also the sort of invective directed against the older
sister as 'past it' which looks forward to the Horace epode quoted
above and poems such as Catullus 41, 43, 58–9.

Some of the invective of Catullus is directed at women, and some
of it is crude. Look for instance at poem 59:

> Bononiensis Rufa Rufulum fellat,
> uxor Meneni, saepe quam in sepulcretis
> uidistis ipso rapere de rogo cenam,

cum deuolutum ex igne prosequens panem
ab semiraso tunderetur ustore.

Bononian Rufa sucks Rufulus off,
the wife of Menenus, whom you have often seen
in graveyards nicking her dinner right off the funeral pyre,
running after a loaf that has rolled out of the fire
and getting banged by the unshaven cremator.

This little story is misogyny in miniature. Rufa is being criticised for
(a) giving oral sex (b) to somebody else's husband then (c) stealing
bread (d) which has been left as offerings in graveyards (e) paying
for it by having sex with the (f) unshaven cremator. The Latin is
much better than any translation could be: notice the juxtaposition
of *Rufa Rufulum* suggesting their physical proximity, the neat touch
uidistis ('you have all seen her so it is not good her denying it'), the
'dinner' which she steals at the end of line 3 turns out to be mere
panem (bread) at the end of line 4, the identity of the meal being
held back while we watch the thing rolling off the fire, her 'chasing'
(*persequens*) following after *deuolutum* (rolling). The Romans used
to burn food and other goods along with the corpse, in the hope
that the dead could use them in the underworld; *ipso* ('right off the
very ...') brings out the indignation at this act of injustice to the
helpless dead. 'Unshaven' (literally 'half-shaved') brings to mind a
mental picture of the scruffy man charged with burning the corpses.
Such men were often slaves or ex-slaves and for Rufa to subject
herself to such a man was therefore highly improper. *Tunderetur*
is nicely ambiguous – it may simply mean 'hit' or it may have the
sexual sense 'banged'. Either way Rufa is being roughly treated by a
slave so that she can steal a loaf of bread from a dead man. It is hard
to imagine more criticism being squeezed into so short a poem.

Ameaena is ridiculed as being the celebrity beauty of the day
when her physical defects are legion – but of course this poem is

possibly more of a love poem for the poet's girlfriend than a direct
attack on a real Ameaena:

> Hello – girl whose nose is not small
> whose foot is not pretty, eyes are not black
> fingers are not long, mouth is not dry
> and a tongue which is certainly not elegant,
> girfriend of the bankrupt from Formiae.
> Is it you that our area reckons is pretty?
> It is you that my Lesbia is compared with?
> What a lack of taste and wit in this generation!
>
>   Poem 43

The real 'point' of the poem is clearly at the end, where the personal
invective against one woman becomes praise of another. In an earlier
poem (41) the poet describes the same girl Ameaena as demanding
a large amount of money from him when she is all too unaware of
how ugly she is – the implication being that she is charging for her
favours and that she is setting her price ridiculously high. The joke
in this poem is that she is asking for money (*aes* in Latin) and yet
really needs to ask the mirror (also called *aes* in Latin).

Most of the invective of Catullus is not directed against women,
however, but men, like the hapless Aemilius whom we smelled at
the start of this chapter. Some of it is gentle humour directed at
associates of the poet – Flavius has a girlfriend but is keeping her
under wraps, which prompts the poet to wonder how hideous she
must be (poem 6). Poem 13 is gentle humour of a particularly skilful
kind:

> cenabis bene, mi Fabulle, apud me
> paucis, si tibi di fauent, diebus,
> si tecum attuleris bonam atque magnam
> cenam, non sine candida puella

et uino et sale et omnibus cachinnis.
haec si, inquam, attuleris, uenuste noster,
cenabis bene; nam tui Catulli
plenus sacculus est aranearum.
sed contra accipies meros amores
seu quid suauius elegantiusue est:
nam unguentum dabo, quod meae puellae
donarunt Veneres Cupidinesque,
quod tu cum olfacies, deos rogabis,
totum ut te faciant, Fabulle, nasum.

You will dine well, my Fabullus, at my house
in a few days, if the Gods are favourable to you,
if you bring with you a good and plentiful
dinner, not without a pretty girl
and wine and sauce and all the guffaws.
If, I say, you bring all this, my dear friend,
you will dine well: for your Catullus'
purse is full of cobwebs.
In return you will get undiluted love
or something more pleasurable and charming:
for I will give you a perfume which the Venuses
and Cupids gave to my girl
and when you smell it you will ask the gods
to make you, Fabullus, all nose.

Note here how the poet keeps the reader guessing. You will have a good dinner at my house – if you bring the food and the girl, that is (so in other words Fabullus could have the dinner at his own house without the poet). Bring *sal* (literally 'salt' but metaphorical for 'wit') and bring lots of laughter. I have a purse that is full – full of spiders. So why come here and not stay at home? What will I give to you in return for all of this? A perfume given by the gods

of love to make you dream of being turned into a giant nose. The
caricature of the addressee being transformed into a walking nose
is the comic punchline of the poem – note the emphatic ending of
the poem with the word *nasum*.

Something similar happens in poem 12:

> Marrucinian Asinius, you do not use your left hand
> nicely; when we are joking and drinking
> you steal the napkins of those who are not watching.
> Do you think this is clever? You are wrong, you fool;
> It is a totally dirty and uncouth thing to do.
> Don't you believe me? Believe Pollio
> your brother, who would like to change
> your thefts and would give a talent to do it;
> he is a boy stuffed full of wit and jokes.
> So either expect three-hundred hendecasyllables
> or send me the napkin back,
> which does not bother me for its price,
> but it is a memento of my friend.
> For Fabullus and Veranius sent me
> Saetaban napkins from Spain as a gift;
> I must love these just as I love
> my little Veranius and Fabullus.

Notice here how the poet begins with innuendo – what is it that
Asinius is doing with his hand at dinner parties? Only in line 3 is
the offence spelled out and this allows the poet to advertise his own
poetic power ('three hundred hendecasyllables') as a threat to the
offender and also to express his affection for his friends Veranius
and Fabullus. Interestingly the offence is one against taste ('dirty
and uncouth') and friendship rather than simply against property,
and the poet responds with a tasteful and elegant poem to set the
man straight.

The poet also holds himself up to mockery in poem 10. Here he describes his embarrassing encounter with a friend's new girlfriend whom he tries to impress by boasting of the property he picked up on the staff of Memmius in Bithynia, only for her to ask him to lend her the sedan chair he describes. He hasn't got one and has to admit this to his burning shame – although he tries to pass it off as forgetfulness. This sort of self-depreciation is perhaps the other side of the coin from the self-deprecating poems 8 and 76 where his inadequacies are of a kind to make him depressed rather than merely embarrassed.

The inadequacy of others in the sexual field is easy prey for the comic poet in Catullus. Look for instance at poem 17, where the whole town is asked to build a bridge so that a particularly foolish cuckold can be thrown from it into the mud for letting his sweet little wife play around and do nothing about it. Once again the comic exaggeration adds to the effect: the wife is 'a girl of the tenderest bloom, more capricious than a sweet little kid, to be looked after more carefully than the blackest of grapes' while her stupid husband is 'a total idiot' who has not got the brains of a 'two-year-old child asleep on the rocking arm of his father'. The man is not just as uninformed as a child, he is as blithely oblivious as a *sleeping* child. So why add that he is 'on the rocking arm of his father'? Perhaps to bring out the comic force of 'two-year-old' with the mental picture of this adult being small enough to fit onto the *ulna* (properly only the forearm) of a father who is rocking him to sleep – unless *tremuli* means rather 'shaking with old age' in which case the (adult) husband is still being rocked to sleep by a feeble aged father. Either way, husband comes out of it very badly. The mud for him to fall into is not just any mud either: notice the exaggeration of the phrasing as the poet spells it out:

> Where of all the lake and the smelly marsh the abyss is
> bluest and deepest.

The Latin is even more gross:

> *uerum totius ut lacus putidaeque paludis*
> *liuidissima maximeque est profunda uorago*

with the expressive words *putidus* (stinking, rotten) and the
superlative *lividissima* to be picked up by *insulsissimus* in the next
line ('most stupid' describing the husband) and showing that one
superlatively stupid man deserves a superlatively blue mud. His fall
is to be one of comic tumbling: he is to fall 'head first into the mud
head over heels' (*ire praecipitem in lutum per caputque pedesque*). He
is compared to a log for his unmoved stolidity, but (again) not just
any old log but

> an alder in a ditch hamstrung by the Ligurian axe

which is comic in that the simile has its own metaphor (logs cannot
literally be 'hamstrung'); and at the end he is compared to a mule
leaving its shoe in the sticky mire. His offence is one of omission
and inability to see what is common knowledge around the town.
Catullus does not name the man or his wife – presumably because
if there were a real case of this kind then all would know the people
concerned anyway and also because the poem stands on its own
merits without needing to be tied to a real topical case.

Sexual failure of a more scandalous kind is the subject matter
of poem 67. The comic character of the poem is made obvious
by the fact that it purports to be a dialogue between a door and
the poet. The form of the poem is that of a rhetorical *diffamatio*
('lampoon') and, for all its spicy colloquialisms, it follows closely
many of the patterns of rhetorical theory and practice. The family
being described is complex to say the least and there are many

loose ends which the poet does not tie up for the reader: are the father and son mentioned in lines 1–6 the same as the incestuous and impotent (respectively) pair in lines 23ff? Why does the door mention Caecilius? Is he the son of Balbus in line 23, or the man with red eyebrows of line 46? To all these questions we can only propose a speculative set of answers, which might be summarised thus: a girl marries a young man who has not the virility to deflower her and so gets his father to do it for him. Once 'broken in' she goes on to have sex with other men in Brixia.

The narrative outlined above can be inferred from the text, and does not sound so promising as a piece of comic poetry. In fact the text is one of considerable subtlety: the sarcastic response at 29–30 neatly marks the end of one tale and the beginning of the next, and the questioning of the door's knowledge at the end (37–41) mirrors the questioning of its probity at the beginning. The registers of language used range widely: the crude ('pissed in his own son's lap' 30), the direct and simple ('committed adultery' 36), the lewd comic description (his 'sword' hung 'floppier than a young beet ...' 21–2), the heavy sarcasm ('an outstanding example of loyalty ...' 29–30), the playful use of unnecessary description of Brixia (32–4), rhetorical question-and-answer both 'real' (15–18) and anticipated (37), didactic manner ('in the first place ...' 19–20), the topically allusive (the tall man with red eyes in lines 45–8) and the morally outraged (24–5). Part of the humour here is the incongruity between form and content, the absurd setting and speaker making the text comic rather than tragic, witty more than it is shocking.

The literary convention of having an inanimate object deliver an address is familiar enough from tombstones ('Traveller, stop and read ...'). This poem is an interesting variation on the 'serenade' (*paraklausithyron*) where the lover, shut out from his beloved's house, speaks to the hard door begging admission, even smearing the step with perfume (Lucretius 4.1177–9; Propertius 1.16; Horace,

Odes 3.10). The poem opens with the language of the serenade, but it soon (5) becomes clear that the speaker has no wish to secure admission but only information (Come now, tell us why ... 7). The door – unlike the dumb and hard doors addressed in the typical serenade – goes on freely to give the information sought and more besides: it is worth pointing out, however, that the speaker both solicits the tale with a moral accusation (5–8) and is himself an agent of gossip ('people say' 3). If the door seems to tell the salacious details with a certain amount of relish, this is to be seen in the tradition of garrulous slaves gossiping in Roman comedy – the door is even described as a slave (5).

The poem is well placed straight after poem 66 where the shorn lock of hair from the head of the Queen Berenice addresses us from the heavens. The door is, like the lock of hair, an inanimate object bound to an owner who knows and reveals personal details about them: the idyllic marriage of Berenice to her heroic husband is in stark contrast to the nameless adulteress in poem 67 whose nominal husband is ridiculously impotent and whose past is anything but fragrant. The lock is a sure sign of the reunion of the married couple, while the door ought to be – but has not been – the safeguard of marital fidelity. The lock was a helpless female in the hands of the brute sword (66.42–50), while Balbus' wife faced no danger at all from her husband's limp 'sword' (*sicula* (21)); the lock refuses offerings from those women who commit adultery (66.84–6), while the door criticises Balbus' wife for similarly committing 'wicked adultery' (*malum ... adulterium* (67.36)). The lock heard the sad words spoken by Berenice to her husband departing for the wars (66.29), while the door heard the wicked wife boasting of her exploits in whispers to her slaves. The mock-heroics of poem 66 here become a savage burlesque of perverted comedy and parodied rhetoric.

The comic effects are obvious in the poem. The limp penis is well described as a 'sword' which 'hung floppier than a young beet and never raised itself to the middle of his tunic' while the father had 'something stiffer to be able to untie her virgin's belt'. The poet responds with a grotesque image of the father 'pissing in his own son's lap' – the deliberate confusion of urination and ejaculation being part of the comic creation and the confusion of whose lap was being entered adding to the scorn. Brixia, it seems, is awash with vice, and the poet and the door use the gossip to create a poem of high entertainment value and some clever poetic effects.

There is abundant mockery of other perverse family relationships as in the following less than charming family group:

> Gallus has brothers. One of them has a very charming
> wife, another has a charming son.
> Gallus is a nice man: for he unites sweet lovers,
> so that pretty girl sleeps with pretty boy.
> Gallus is a fool, and doesn't see that he has a wife,
> and that he the uncle is showing how to cuckold an uncle.
>   Poem 78

The reader will be puzzled by the sexual family-tree here depicted. That is of course the point – the family goes in for incest on a truly mind-blowing scale – but it also allows the poet to indulge his taste for paradox and clever use of language. What makes the tale even more insidious is the fairytale beginning and the way the poet manages to avoid obscenity in his depiction of incest. The poet's pose is of moral outrage, telling a shocking tale of 'sophisticated' sexual manners in a style reminiscent of a children's story. Similar is this poem:

> Gellius, what is that man doing, who lusts with mother and
>   sister
> and does it all night with clothes thrown off?
> What is he doing, who does not let his uncle have a wife?

do you know how great a crime he is undertaking?
He is undertaking one so big that not even furthest Tethys
washes away, nor Oceanus father of the Nymphs:
for there is no crime that he could move into beyond this
   one,
not even if he lowered his head and swallowed himself.
      Poem 88

The poem ends with the suitably cartoon-like image of a man fellating himself, made all the more effectively bathetic by following the 'high' style of the preceding lines with their mention of sea-deities. What is even more striking here is that this piece of grossly obscene gossip manages to use not one single obscene word. This Gellius is also mocked in the following poem 89 for the lean physique which his excessive sexual activity has given him; in poem 80 his white lips are explained as the result of his fellating another man. The pose of righteous indignation resurfaces in the critique of Aufillena:

Aufillena, to live content with one man only
is the highest praise of all praise for wives;
but it is better to go to bed with anybody at all
than to be a mother giving birth to cousins from your own
   uncle.
      Poem 111

Here traditional wifely virtue is praised – the epithet *univira* (only married to one man throughout her life) is found on tombstones – only to present the monstrous immorality of this wife in the starkest terms. Again the last line is one of head-scratching paradox – in Latin the line reads *quam matrem fratres ex patruo parere* ('than mother cousins from uncle to get') and the word *fratres* (here meaning cousins) also more commonly means 'brothers' which only adds to the confusion.

Confusion is perhaps the point. It is hard to believe that the poet 'sincerely' disapproved so much of the sexual shenanigans of comparative strangers and much easier to see this sort of poetry as affecting a stance of moral disapproval whose main theme is comic. Sexual misbehaviour may be extremely vicious in some cases, but the poet's purpose here is surely to elicit humour and show wit rather than to produce letters to the press.

Look also at the next poem in the collection:

> You're a great man, Naso, and there's not a great number of
>   men who don't
> fuck you. Naso, you're a great guy and a pansy.
>
>   Poem 112

The Latin word *multus* is used three times in this two-line poem and much of the wit of the poem relies on it. Naso is a 'great' or 'big' man but he prefers to allow himself to be penetrated by others rather than to use his 'largeness' in more standard masculine ways. Here again is the disapproval of 'fake men who try to attract other men' (as Ovid later described the male homosexual in his *Art of Love* 1.524), the sense that it is somehow permissible for a male to seek to kiss and penetrate a boy like Iuventius but for a grown man to be sodomised by another is the greatest shame he could incur.

More acceptable to modern sensibility perhaps is the gentle ribbing at a man's mannerisms, such as Arrius' insistence of starting words with an 'h' sound (so he would say 'hadvantages' for 'advantages'); this poem manages to include examples of Arrius' mistaken pronunciation at the beginning and end of lines, ending with the climactic word which so sums up Arrius' mistake:

> *chommoda* dicebat, si quando commoda uellet
>   dicere, et insidias Arrius *hinsidias*,
> et tum mirifice sperabat se esse locutum,

cum quantum poterat dixerat hinsidias.
credo, sic mater, sic semper auunculus eius,
   sic maternus auus dixerat atque auia.
hoc misso in Syriam requierant omnibus aures:
   audibant eadem haec leniter et leuiter,
nec sibi postilla metuebant talia uerba,
   cum subito affertur nuntius horribilis,
Ionios fluctus, postquam illuc Arrius isset,
   iam non Ionios esse sed *Hionios*.

Arrius used to say 'hadvantages' if ever he wanted to say
advantages, and 'hambush' for 'ambush',
and then he hoped that he had spoken impressively
when he had said 'hambush' with all the force at his
   disposal.
I believe that is how his mother had always spoken, and his
   uncle,
and his maternal grandfather and grandmother too.
When this man was sent to Syria everybody's ears had a rest;
they heard these same things smoothly and softly,
nor did they fear such words afterwards,
when suddenly a dreadful messenger is brought in:
The Ionian waves, after Arrius had gone there,
were no longer 'Ionian' but 'Hionian'.
                   Poem 84

Look also at the mockery of Egnatius whose suspiciously white
teeth are the result of his drinking his own urine (poem 39). He
is so proud of his teeth that he beams a brilliant smile even on
the least appropriate occasions such as a funeral, thus combining
social ineptitude with his eccentric oral hygiene. Furius is similarly
mocked in poem 22 for the dryness of his family diet resulting in
his shitting pebbles.

Political satire is something which we might expect from this urbane poet. Well-known figures of contemporary Rome ought to find themselves in the firing line for his scathing attacks. What is interesting about those poems which deal with political celebrities is that there is no trace of any political feeling here but merely personal abuse. One famous example is the poem addressed to the lawyer and politician Cicero:

> Most eloquent of the descendants of Romulus,
> all that are, all that have been, Marcus Tullius,
> and all that will be in years to come;
> Catullus the worst poet of them all
> pays you the greatest thanks;
> he is as much the worst poet of all
> as you are the best patron of all.
>
> Poem 49

Apparent praise of the great man may well here be masking mockery – the text assumes that the poet admires Cicero as much as he regards himself as 'worst of all poets'. The inference to be drawn is that this is subtle satire of Cicero, whose status as the 'best patron of all' suggests that he would produce this sort of lavish and fulsome oratory for anybody who paid him. The poet covers his tracks with the apparent meaning of the poem – but leaves an undercurrent of humour for the discerning to read behind the praise.

A more obvious target of the poet's satire is Julius Caesar, the general and politician who was in the 50s BCE building up a reputation and a power base which would see him created dictator and then assassinated in the following decade. Poem 93 is addressed to him:

> Caesar, I am not overkeen to want to please you,
> nor to know whether you are a white man or black.

The poem is as tiny as the poet's regard for Caesar is tiny; and yet real disregard for an individual does not compose poems at all, however short. The studied indifference to one who exercised enormous power is not confirmed by the poet's interest in Caesar's sex life with his boyfriend:

> They make a good pair, the shameless perverts
> Mamurra and bumboy Caesar.
> And no wonder – both of them has the same black marks
> one from the city, the other from Formiae,
> stamped on them for good and will not be washed away
> equally diseased, a pair of identical twins,
> both of them little scholars on the one same couch,
> neither of them more greedy for sex than the other,
> rival mates of the little girlies.
> They make a good pair, the shameless perverts.
>
> Poem 57

Suetonius in his *Life of Caesar* (73) tells us that Catullus had libelled Caesar in his poetry; Caesar accepted that these amounted to a permanent stain on his name but also accepted Catullus' apology and even invited him to dinner. So what is going on in this poem? Caesar and his associate Mamurra are said to be sexual perverts (with Caesar adopting the passive position in the sodomy); they are said to have less than distinguished origins and they are said to share intellectual pretensions (as 'little scholars'). They have sex with each other but also pursue girls young enough to be their children (Caesar is said to have had the daughters as well as the wives of other men, according to Suetonius *Life of Caesar* 50). All in all they are a pair of weak and shameless men in their sex lives and pretentious about their social origins and their intellectual capacities. Nothing about politics, however.

We see a lot of Mamurra in the poems, in fact and he seems to have given him the unpleasant soubriquet *Mentula* ('prick') to add to the mockery. The man in question was a well-to-do man from Formiae in South Latium, close colleague of Caesar in Spain in 61 BCE and then later in Gaul. That his acquisition and consumption of wealth was a scandal in Rome is confirmed by Cicero (*Letters to* Atticus 7.7.6); and his house became a byword in luxurious living. The reason for the poet's hostility to this man may be personal – there are several references to a 'bankrupt from Formiae' in connection with Ameaena, for instance – or it may simply be that he was an easy target. He is abused for his attempts to write poetry (105), his pretence of being a rich landowner (114–5) and his adultery (94). Poem 29 is a longer and less jolly poem about Mamurra and verges on political satire:

> Who can see this, who can allow it –
> unless he is shameless and greedy and a gambler –
> Mamurra having all that Long-haired Gaul
> and furthest Britain used to have before?
> Queer Romulus, will you see this and endure it?
> Will he now, proud and prodigal,
> walk round the marriage-beds of everybody
> like a white dove or Adonis?
> Queer Romulus, will you see this and endure it?
> You are shameless, greedy and a gambler.
> Was it on that account, o general without peer,
> that you were on the furthest island of the west,
> so that that shagged-out prick of yours
> might gobble up twenty or thirty million?
> If that isn't idiotic generosity, then what is?
> Has he not screwed and gourmandised enough already?
> First his father's goods were mangled,
> then the Pontic loot, then thirdly

the Spanish stuff which the gold-bearing river Tagus knows:
is it he who now has the best bits of Gaul and Britain?
Why the hell do you nurture this man? What can he do
except gobble up fat inheritances?
Is that the reason, o holiest men of the city,
father-in-law and son-in-law, that you have wasted
     everything?

The father-in-law is Caesar, whose daughter Julia was married
to Pompey the great until her death in 54 BCE; they – as senior
politicians in this period – are being blamed for the way in which
Mamurra has been allowed to squander whole fortunes, partly
while he was acting as Caesar's chief engineer in his campaigns
in Lusitania (modern Portugal). The 'furthest island in the west'
refers to Britain, which Caesar came to in 55 and 54 BCE; while the
phrase 'shagged-out prick' (*diffututa mentula*) probably confirms
that this man is one and the same as 'Prick' in other poems. The
addressee of the poem is called 'Queer Romulus' and may refer to
either Pompey or Caesar; what is interesting here is that the poet
does not spell out the identification of the man and perhaps the
term was topical at the time when the poem was composed. Once
again, however, one wonders how seriously to take the poem as a
piece of satire. The image of the 'prick' eating up whole fortunes
is comic, as is the picture of the man walking nonchalantly round
the bedrooms of the Romans like an Adonis. The practice of satire
could be briefly summed up: first simplify and then exaggerate.
Catullus does this ably here. The message is very simple – Mamurra
is taking more than he is entitled to – and the comic exaggeration
is plain to see. Like much Roman satire, Catullus' scornful invective
can come over as pompous and deliberately absurd, a creation of a
moralistic tirade which amuses more than it shocks. One wonders
what the poets would write about if there were no Gellius types or

Mamurras to mock. The feeling behind these poems is one of both amusement and also power as the great and the rich of the Roman world are ridiculed down to pathetic size by the power of the poet's wit and humour.

The tradition lived on – most notably in the work of the later poet Martial, whose exuberant and scathing poems owe much of their style and their power to Catullus. Look for instance at 11.6 where Martial quotes Catullus directly:

> Give me kisses now – but Catullan ones: if they are as many as he said, then I will give you the sparrow of Catullus.

He also quotes (11.20) some verses written by Augustus Caesar about the wife of his enemy Mark Antony, Fulvia:

> Read six verses of Augustus Caesar, you grumpy man, you who can only read Latin words with a long face:

>> Because Antony fucks Glaphyra, Fulvia has settled this punishment for me – that I should fuck her. Me to fuck Fulvia? What if Manius asked me to bugger him, would I do it? I think not. 'Fuck me or let's fight' she says. But what of the fact that my prick is dearer to me than life itself? Let the battle begin!

> Augustus, you pardon my witty little books – you know how to speak with Roman clarity.

The short verse epigram which Catullus used to such devastating effect was clearly a form which Romans of his own day and of subsequent generations found to be a weapon worth delivering.

CHAPTER 6

FIRST AND LAST THINGS

This chapter will look at the arrangement of the poems in the book, and the significance of the first and last poems in the collection, as well as examining some of the ways in which the poet signals closure in his text.

The ordering of the poems is worth discussing. The 116 poems which make up the book are ordered in three clear groups: the poems in a variety of metres, followed by the 'long poems' 61–8, followed by 69–116 which are all composed in elegiac couplets. Within the overarching metrical groupings, however, the poems are ordered in such a way as to provide continuity and variety in equal measures. Poems 5 and 7 are similar love poems, the later one being something of a sequel to the earlier poem, but in between them comes poem 6 which is looking critically at the love-life of Flavius; this gives us an ironic view of the poet himself by comparison and contrast with Flavius who is to Catullus as 'Catullus' is to us in poems 5 and 7. Poem 96 is a highly charged and emotional consolation to the bereaved Calvus but is at once followed by the scatological excess of poem 97 (Aemilius' smelly mouth), almost as if the reader is being urged that life must go on. The persona of the poet changes from poem to poem in a pleasingly ironic manner, so that for instance the criticism of adultery in poem 61.97–9 rings oddly when we see the celebration of adultery in 68.145–6. There are groups of poems within the collection so that one can extract the Lesbia poems, the Iuventius poems and so on, but the reader is not allowed to dwell on one individual for too long and monotony and predictability are always avoided. The love celebrated in poems 107 and 109 is separated by the savage violence of poem 108 and followed by a poem reproaching a certain Aufilena for not giving Catullus the sex she had promised; the happy love of poem 7 is countered by the misery of lost love in poem 8. Within the long poems 61–8 there are again common themes and strands running through: the theme of marriage as celebrated happily in poems 61 and 62, subverted ironically in poem 64, and turned upside down in poem 68 where the lover is married to another man and stolen by the poet and in poem 67 where the bride is deflowered by her own father-in-law. The happy marriage of Berenice and Ptolemy in poem 66 looks back to the wedding songs poems 61 and 62 and also forward to that of Laudamia and Protesilaus in poem 68, contrasted with the unhappy unions in poems 64 and 67.

Poem 1

The first poem in a collection is always important if the poet wishes his readers to be enticed into the book. The first poem in the Book of Catullus is both a preface and a dedication, a programme and an apologia. It is addressed to Cornelius Nepos (110–24 BCE), a contemporary and fellow countryman of the poet, of whose massive output only fragments and some brief biographical essays survive. Nepos does not shine in the eyes of more modern critics: Horsfall in the *Cambridge History of Classical Literature* (vol. 2 p. 116) describes Nepos as an 'intellectual pygmy' and the latest edition of the *Oxford Classical Dictionary* lists his faults as 'hasty and careless composition and lack of control of his material ... As historian his value is slight ... his style is plain.' There is one reference to Catullus in the surviving works of Nepos, when he names Catullus and Lucretius the most significant poets of the generation (*Atticus* 12.4), which at least shows that the historian knew and rated the poet. Why did Catullus choose to dedicate his book to such a man?

It was of course conventional to dedicate a book of poetry to a named individual. Lucretius dedicates the *de rerum natura* to Memmius and addresses him by name, just as Hesiod had addressed his laggard brother Perses in his *Works and Days*. Horace and Virgil both dedicate poetry to Maecenas and this is surely a sign that Maecenas was their patron in a more or less materialistic sense. The fact that literary patronage lived alongside and subsumed political patronage is something which makes us wonder how independent a writer could dare to be in a world where he who paid the piper called the tune. Poets might feel obliged to compose laudatory poetry to praise the families of their patrons and also be steered towards the sorts of literature which the literary and social elite favoured. Now of course there are plenty of 'refusal poems' (*recusationes*) in which the poet apologises for his inability or disinclination to compose the sort of poem which his patron desires – poems which both assert the persuasive power of the patron and also undermine it. There is also the consideration that poets – unlike less exalted *clientes* – have something very big to offer their patrons in return for patronage. Poets can (after all) immortalise the name of the patron in verse, and the somewhat meretricious nature of the relationship should not blind us to the fact that Pindar was (presumably) paid for his poetry and yet is no mere sycophantic court poet. Under the Roman empire the hands of the poet would be tied more closely to the wishes of his emperor, but in the world of Catullus the patronage seems more loose and almost informal. Later patrons – such as Caius Asinius Pollio who was one of the patrons of Horace and who founded the first public library in Rome – were men of culture and political eminence who saw literature as both a pleasure and a useful adjunct to their armour.

The role of Nepos in this poem is, then, one of literary rather than political significance. He is described as having composed a giant history of the world in three rolls, a tremendous feat of diligence; this is in sharp contrast to Catullus, whose 'little trifles' are not big, and who wrote in verse rather than prose. Poet and patron share the quality of *doctrina* as discussed above in chapter four – Nepos produced work in rolls which were 'learned and hard work'.

Otherwise the focus of the poem is on the poetry itself and it acts almost as a shop window for the rest of the collection. Look at the very first line:

Cui dono lepidum nouum libellum

To whom am I giving this new elegant little book ...?

Note the emphasis on smallness of scale (*little* book), on elegance (*lepos* is a word of praise in many of the poems here) and of course on 'newness' – these were after all the poets whom Cicero termed the Neoterics. The neatness of expression is then conveyed in the next line in the punning metaphor 'polished off with dry pumice'. 'Polishing off' could either be literal – Roman books were written on papyrus rolls, whose ends were polished with the dry pumice stone – or literary polishing of the material. 'Dry' is also a term of criticism applied to speech or writing which is tedious or grating – thus allowing Catullus the paradox that the 'dry' stone will produce what is anything but 'dry'. The poet's modesty is repeated ('you thought my trifles were worth something ... have this book, whatever it is worth ...') in an ironic study of playfulness when we know that many of the poems here represent far more effort than that of mere *jeux d'esprit* and probably more than the three rolls of Nepos' *Chronika*. Irony – in the original sense of 'mock-modesty' as in the Ironic Man in Theophrastus' *Characters* – is often a mask behind which the writer peeps out at his audience, or a way of drawing attention to the artist as well as the art. It is also a way of teasing the reader who does not know at this stage what to make of a poet opening his collection with a disavowal of their literary merit.

Closure

If the first poem in the book looks forward and entices the reader into the text, then every poem after this one has in some way to mark itself off as complete and force the reader to look back. The poet's desire to provide 'closure' has been much discussed in recent years, and we have seen some fascinating examples earlier on, of the ways in which Catullus manages to mark the end of a poem without a bland 'and therefore' conclusion. Closure is a vital framing device, acting almost like the poet's signature at the end of a piece. Think back to the end of poem 64 for instance, where a brilliant mythological epyllion concludes with a wry moralistic epilogue blaming the absence of the gods in contemporary Rome on the impiety and immortality of the Romans; hardly the ending one expects and leaving the reader scratching his head in bafflement at the 'message' while also marvelling at the way in which the poet has concluded with the themes of the poem (light, human sacrifice, marriage) all being tied together and encapsulated in a wonderful final couplet:

> Quare nec talis dignantur visere coetus
> Nec se contingi patiuntur lumine claro

> (and so they do not deem our unions worthy of seeing
> nor do they let themselves be touched by the clear light of
> day)

which has the 'and so' phrase wrapping the poem up and then picks up the key elements of sexual union (*coetus*) of seeing (as Ariadne was seen by Bacchus as she saw Theseus departing, as Thetis first saw Peleus, as the Argonauts first saw the sea nymphs) and the clarity of the light which illuminates all. One has the sense of a recapitulation of the story and also an air of finality as the poet brings the mythical past right up to date with a self-referential epilogue showing the contemporary world visited by no gods. The poem thus ends, in a sense, with the poet and his frail world looking in wonder at the creation he has just written. Poem 63 ends with a similar modern twist as the poet prays to be spared the sort of madness which so injured Attis. Over many of the poems looms the finality of death: remember the poet's urgent address to 'Lesbia' in poem 5 to love while we can because eternal death is on its way, and look at the wonderfully plangent lament for the poet's dead brother:

> Through many peoples and carried across many seas
> I come to these sad burial rites, brother,
> so that I might endow you with the final gift of death
> and address your silent ashes to no purpose.
> Since fortune has robbed me of you yourself.
> Alas, sad brother unworthily stolen from me,
> But at any rate now receive these rites, which in the
>   ancestral custom
> of our parents have been handed down as a bitter gift at
>   funerals,
> rites flowing much with brotherly weeping,
> and, brother, for all time, hail and farewell.
>   Poem 101

The repetitions so common in funeral lament are there (many ... many) as is the constant harking on the fraternal relationship ('brother ... sad brother ... brotherly ... brother') and the family customs being duly performed (lines 7–8). The carrying out of rituals laid down by the ancestors is something for the poet to hold on to in his (otherwise) despairing grief (look at his use of the word *nequiquam* 'to no purpose', and his description of the ashes as 'silent'). The poem thus brings out the distance involved – over many lands and seas is a literal distance, while the yawning gulf between the living and the dead is even further – and also the closeness of the two brothers. The pain of grief is underlined by this image of the closest of brothers being separated by a limitless abyss. The final closure of death is here treated with enormous pathos and human empathy – as it is also handled in the consolation to Calvus on the death of his wife in poem 96 – and the death of the poet's brother is dovetailed beautifully into the texture of poem 68 which both laments the sorrow of death and also celebrates the joys of life, seeing the darkness and the light, and ending with the depiction of his married lover as 'my light, whose life makes living sweet'. Life, in this case, overcomes the closure of death, as poem 5 had urged.

Other poems gain closure by a wry twist. This might be humourous – as Fabullus praying to become one big nose in poem 13, or the money / mirror pun in poem 41, or the 'mouth-fucking' at the end of poem 21 where Aurelius is threatened with oral sex if he touches the poet's boyfriend – the joke being that Aurelius is stingy with his food and reluctant to feed himself and so needs something putting into his mouth. Poem 39 examines the gleaming smile of Egnatius, beaming at all on the most inappropriate occasions; the poet ends with the grotesque reason why Egnatius' teeth are so white. Poem 88 ends with the gross image of Gellius fellating himself. Some poems end with a generalizing comment (poems 22, 45) while impersonal poems such as poem 64 end (as we saw above) with a personal touch; conversely the personal poem 70 ends with a generalised impersonal ending:

> My woman says that she would prefer to marry nobody else but me, not even if Jupiter himself asked her.

That's what she says – but what a woman says to her
    ardent lover
Deserves to be written on the wind and the fast-running
    water.

Other poems mark their ending with ring-composition: poem 16 has the first line repeated at the end, while poem 99 recalls the opening line in its final promise never again to steal kisses.

Endgame

As we have seen, the poet keeps his readers on their toes by foiling their expectations and not allowing them to guess what is coming next. He keeps us in suspense even in the very final poem.

saepe tibi studioso animo uenante requirens
    carmina uti possem mittere Battiadae,
qui te lenirem nobis, neu conarere
    tela infesta <meum> mittere in usque caput,
hunc uideo mihi nunc frustra sumptum esse laborem,
    Gelli, nec nostras hic ualuisse preces.
contra nos tela ista tua euitabimus acta
    at fixus nostris tu dabis supplicium.

I have often searched diligently, hunting out
How I might be able to send you poems of Callimachus,
So as to soften you towards me and stop you from trying
To fire weapons of wrath at my head.
I now see that this labour of mine was undertaken in vain,
Gellius, and that my prayers in this regard were powerless.
So in return for this I will avoid those weapons which you
    have fired;
But you will pay the penalty for this, stabbed by me.

On the face of it, this poem seems to mark an ending of an attitude: no more Mr Nice Guy – the poet will not try to placate Gellius any more with his poems. The poet has indeed launched many an attack on Gellius in the preceding 115 poems (74, 80, 88–91) and so the pose of hurt and wounded sensitivity ('to stop you from trying to fire weapons ...') may be consciously ironic from a poet who can always give as good as he gets. The poem has a lot of interesting features: the third line is that rarest of rare birds, a hexameter line entirely made up of long syllables, and is possibly a mockery of Gellius' 'rustic' manner of speaking. The first six lines make up one long sentence with the imagery of hunting at the forefront of the poet's mind ('hunting ... fire weapons at my head'); the thrust of the poem is that the poet / victim / hunted will end up being the hunter (Gellius will be stabbed). Behind the 'hunting' metaphor in line one is of course the simple point that finding the right words to translate difficult Greek into elegant Latin requires hunting through the language. It is difficult, however, to see in what sense this poem acts as final poem to end the collection.

Now of course it may well be that the poems were not ordered by the poet; or that other poems followed this one but were subsequently lost. But if this is the final poem in Catullus' book – and there is no evidence that it is not – then we have a duty as critics to find reasons to support its position. Colin Macleod in a famous article on the poem[7] showed that it is an 'inverted dedication': 'dedicatory poems tend to speak of the work which goes into the poetry (e.g. Lucretius 1.52, 140–5), of the poet's desire to honour (e.g. poem 1) or acquire (Lucretius 1.140–1) a friendship',[8] whereas this poem looks back on such efforts as a waste of time and determines to hit back. There is ring-composition in the echoes of poem 1 in this concluding poem: Nepos thought that Catullus' little trifles were worth something, while Catullus claims here that his efforts were pointless. Both poems refer to the effort involved in presenting and creating the poems (poem 1 speaks of the book as being 'polished up' while poem 116 speaks of his 'diligent search') and both refer one way or another to Callimachus – implicitly in the evaluative terms used in poem 1 (*lepidum* (elegant) being especially a Callimachean term) and explicitly in the name *Battiadae* in poem 116 ('scion of Battus' referring to Callimachus who came from Cyrene founded by Battus). In poem 1 the poet praises the hard work of his patron, while in poem 116 he speaks of his own *laborem*. What distinguishes poem 116 from other 'epilogue poems' such as Horace, *Odes* 3.30, which openly describe and defend the poetry collection which they conclude, is that this poem does so obliquely, with some degree of retrospection but with the upbeat note that there is much more to come. This sort of 'false closure' epilogue is not unknown in later poets but is something of a pioneering move in Catullus.

The text is typically Catullus in that it foils our expectations of a conclusion while still providing one. We expect a summing up of the achievement of the book and find a dismissive sneer and a sense that work is still very much in progress. The reader is invited to recall two key elements of the poetry, the twin poles of the 'aesthete and the mudslinger' in Macleod's terms, harking back to the Callimachean work such as poem 66 and also to the invective contained in the poems attacking such men as Gellius and Mamurra. This poet is not, however, going into retirement just yet – a point made clear by the present tense of the participle *requirens* ('hunting') in line 1. The style is also self-conscious and sophisticated; Gellius might use a rough manner of speech as shown in the spondaic line 3, and deliver 'weapons', but Catullus produces poetry (*carmina*) in response, and Catullus is a peacemaker with prayers while Gellius is a warrior aiming weapons at the poet's head.

And after that? There is an attractive theory put forward by T.P. Wiseman[9] that Catullus went on to write mimes – we do know of a writer of mimes with the name Catullus and it is always possible that the young man who wrote his lyric and elegiac poems in his youth went on to work for the stage – but here as in so many areas of Catullus' poetry we run into the vacuum of information. We are left in the end with nothing but the poems themselves, which, baffling and fragmentary as so many of them are, still speak to every generation of readers with the freshness of poetry composed only yesterday. They succeed because they manage to bridge the divide between ancient and modern, between past and present, between us and them. They are a window into the world of Roman poetry but also a mirror in which we see our own souls and feelings reflected.

Notes

Chapter 1

1 *Cambridge History of Classical Literature* vol. 2 (1982) p. 12.
2 Wiseman, T.P., *Catullus and His World* (1985) p. 126.
3 See Swain in Holford-Strevens and Vardi, *The Worlds of Aulus Gellius* (2004) pp. 3–40.
4 See Griffin, J., *Latin Poets and Roman Life* (1985) ch. 1.
5 See Ogilivie, *The Romans and Their Gods* (1969) p. 17–19.

Chapter 2

6 If that is what the phrase *ilia rumpens* means. There is much debate about this term which literally means 'breaking the groins'

Chapter 6

7 Macleod, C.W., 'Catullus 116' *Classical Quarterly* 23 (1973) pp. 304–9.
8 art.cit, p. 308.
9 Wiseman, T.P., *Catullus and his World* (1985) pp. 192–8, 258.

Further reading

Chapter 1

Catullus has been translated and edited many times. Some modern English editions of the text include (*indicates that the text is translated into English):

Mynors, R.A.B. (Oxford Classical Text, 1958)

Fordyce, C.J. (Oxford, 1961)

Quinn, K. (London, 1970)

Thomson, D.F.S. (Chapel Hill, 1978)

*Whigham, P., *The Poems of Catullus* (Penguin, 1980)

*Goold, G.P. (London, 1983) (text and facing translation)

*Lee, G. (Oxford, 1990) (translation only, with notes)

Garrison, D.H. (London, 1991)

*Godwin, J., *Poems 61–68* (Warminster, 1995: text and facing translation, commentary)

*Godwin, J., *The Shorter Poems* (Warminster, 1999: text and facing translation, commentary)

*Balmer, Josephine, *Catullus: Poems of Love and Hate* (Bloodaxe Press, 2004)

*Green, P., *The Poems of Catullus: a bilingual edition* (Berkeley: University of California Press, 2005; text and translation with explanatory notes).

For a wide range of translations of Catullus into English, see:
Gaisser, Julia Haig, *Catullus in English* (London, 2001)

Websites with links to further information about the poet include:

Bibliography: http://www.gltc.leidenuniv.nl/index.php3?c=127

http://www.poetry-archive.com/c/catullus_bibliography.html

http://www.let.kun.nl/~m.v.d.poel/bibliografie/catullus.htm

An electronic text of the Latin can be found at: http://www.thelatinlibrary. com/

The Perseus website (http://www.perseus.tufts.edu/cache/perscoll_Greco-Roman.html) has text with several translations and morphological links.

The Classics Pages website even has some Catullus poems read aloud in Latin and can be found at: http://www.classicspage.com/

The vroma site has texts of Catullus with facing literal translations at: http://www.vroma.org/~hwalker/VRomaCatullus/list.html

This site can translate any Catullus poem into any one of 27 modern languages: http://rudy.negenborn.net/catullus/text2/l1.htm

For a good survey of Catullus' life and times see T.P. Wiseman, *Catullus and his World; a Reappraisal* (Cambridge, 1985).

For the background to Roman literary culture in Catullus' time see E.J. Kenney's 'Books and Readers in the Roman World' in *The Cambridge History of Classical Literature* vol. 2 part 1 pp. 3–32; Ogilvie, *Roman Literature and Society* (London, 1991) pp. 11–99 or Elaine Fantham's *Roman Literary Culture* (Johns Hopkins, 1999) pp. 1–54. The background to the survival of the text is well covered in Reynolds and Wilson's *Scribes and Scholars* (2nd edition 1991, Oxford University Press). The 3rd edition of the *Oxford Classical Dictionary* (1996) has excellent summaries and reference material (with bibliographical suggestions) on all the authors and topics discussed in this chapter.

Chapter 2

The conventional view of the Neoterics and their place in Roman poetry is given by Kenneth Quinn in both *The Catullan Revolution* (Cambridge, 1959) and later *Catullus; an Interpretation* (London, 1972). The picture of a 'revolution' in Roman poetry at this time has been critically discussed by Stephen Hinds, *Allusion and Intertext* (Cambridge, 1998) pp. 74–83 and Llewellyn Morgan in Taplin (ed.), *Literature in the Greek and Roman Worlds* (Oxford, 2000) pp. 349–58.

On Plato and the imagery of poetic madness see Murray, *Plato on Poetry* (Cambridge, 1996) pp. 6–12. For more information on Alexandrian and Hellenistic Literature such as that which so influenced Catullus and his circle, see *The Cambridge History of Classical Literature* vol. 1 ch. 18, or Suzanne Said and Monique Trédé's *A Short History of Greek Literature* (London, 1999) pp. 95–109. A fuller account is given in Gregory Hutchinson's *Hellenistic Poetry* (Oxford, 1988).

Chapter 3

For the Roman Life of Love see (e.g.) R.O.A.M. Lyne, *The Latin Love Poets* (Oxford, 1980, revised 1996) ch. 1; J. Griffin, *Latin Poets and Roman Life* (London, 1985) and Susan Treggiari, *Roman Marriage* (Oxford, 1991).

For a full discussion of the identity of Lesbia see T.P. Wiseman, *Catullan Questions* (Leicester, 1969) pp. 51–60.

For the similes in poem 68 see the article by Denis Feeney 'Shall I compare thee ...?: Catullus 68a and the limits of analogy' in Woodman and Powell, *Author and Audience in Latin Literature* (Cambridge, 1992) pp. 33–44.

Chapter 4

On Catullus 64 there is a large literature. One or two pieces stand out as especially worth reading: Richard Jenkyns' *Three Classical Poets* ch. 2 ('Catullus and the Idea of a Masterpiece'); Andrew Laird, 'Art and Text in Catullus 64' in the *Journal of Roman Studies* (1993) pp. 18–30. Amanda Kolson Hurley's *Catullus* (London, 2004) has a whole chapter ('The artist in a fallen world' pp. 96–114) devoted to poem 64.

I have discussed Catullus 63 in more detail in my edition of the longer poems, *Catullus poems 61–68* (Warminster, 1995).

Chapter 5

On Aristophanes see K.J. Dover, *Aristophanic Comedy* (London, 1972). Specifically on Aristophanes' use of obscenity (and not for the squeamish) is J. Henderson, *The Maculate Muse: Obscene Language in Attic Comedy* (Oxford, 1991). For the detailed discussion of obscene terms in Latin see J.N. Adams, *The Latin Sexual Dictionary* (London, 1982) and for their use in Roman Literature see Amy Richlin's *The Garden of Priapus: Sexuality and Aggression in Roman Humour* (Oxford, 1983, revised 1992).

On Satire see e.g. S.H. Braund, *Roman Verse Satire* (Oxford, 1982); N. Rudd, *The Satires of Horace* (Cambridge, 1966); M. Coffey, *Roman Satire* (London, 1976); K. Freudenberg, *Satires of Rome: Threatening Poses from Lucilius to Juvenal* (Cambridge, 2001).

For more discussion of Catullus' invective and humour see W. Fitzgerald, *Catullan Provocations: Lyric Poetry and the Drama of Position* (California, 1995).

For the work of Martial see the selection of his epigrams (Latin text with full commentary) by Lindsay and Patricia Watson (Cambridge, 2003); a shorter selection (with translation by James Michie) is available in the Penguin Classics series.

Chapter 6

For the world of Roman patronage see e.g. A. Wallace-Hadrill (ed.), *Patronage in Ancient Society* (London, 1990); J. Griffin's masterly essay 'Augustus and the Poets: *Caesar qui cogere posset*' in Millar and Segal, *Caesar Augustus; Seven Aspects* (Oxford, 1984) pp. 189–218; E. Fantham, *Roman Literary Culture* (Johns Hopkins, 1996) pp. 67–84.

Index of Passages

INDEX
OF CATULLUS POEMS

Poem number followed by the page(s) on which each poem appears

GENERAL INDEX